For the love

A Quarantine-inspired Cookbook bringing families together

With thanks

Thank you to my sweet family for putting up with countless new recipes and some epic fails and for their patience in making this happen.
Quarantine wouldn't have been the same without you!

Copyright © 2020 Melinda McAlindon

All rights reserved. This book or any portion thereof may not be reproduced or used in any manner whatsoever without the express written permission of the publisher except for the use of brief quotations in a book review.

Printed in United States

ISBN: (8x8 Hardcover)
        978-1-735-70940-6 (Larger Print Hardcover)
        978-0-578-75256-3 (ebook)
        978-1-7357094-1-3 (8.5x8.5 softcover)

Library of Congress Control Number: 2020915770

First printing 2020.
           America First Publishing
           100 Monroe Street
           Centerton, AR, 72719
           www.forthelovecookbook.com

CONTENTS

- **2** Introduction
- **5** Starters & Beverages
- **23** Salads & Sides
- **41** Breads
- **51** Main Dishes
- **131** Desserts
- **143** Appendix
- **148** Index of Recipes

INTRODUCTION

I never planned to write a cookbook, but then again, I never planned to be quarantined for 3 months! But as moms do, I decided to make lemonade.

My college student was on spring break with a couple of friends when the initial stages of quarantine hit. She came home with one of her friends, an exchange student from the Bahamas, for two weeks of "flattening the curve".

When curve flattening turned into extended quarantine, our sweet exchange student became another family member. Suddenly we were a family of seven, including 4 teens, eating three meals a day, every day at the house. Now that's a lot of cooking!

Cooking, for me, is love. It's one of the many ways I care for my family and it's fun. But, as covid hit our little town in NW Arkansas, we did our best to stay positive and entertained. We played games, painted with Bob Ross, completed jigsaw puzzles (minus the piece we lost) and caught up on books and movies. After a couple of weeks of cooking, I became bored. How many groundhog days can one person experience? It was at that point I decided that we would not be repeating a meal throughout covid –

every meal would be a new experience. Had I known it would last for nearly 3 months, perhaps I would not have been so adamant. As we searched and created new meals, we experienced such variety of flavors!

This book is a collection of those dishes. In addition to recipes for appetizers, sides and desserts, I selected exactly 40 of our favorite main meals.

Why 40? Well, in the 14th century, Europe was fighting the plague. Countries recognized that diseases were being brought into their country through the many ships that arrived at port. Italy, specifically, decided that ships had to remain off shore for a period of time to protect the port cities from disease. Likely, because 40 is so significant in the bible, Noah and the ark, and Jesus in the desert, they determined that 40 days would be the perfect amount of time. Any guesses what 40 is in Italian?

Quaranta!
So the off shore period became known as **Quarantine**.

I hope you enjoy this cookbook. It is certainly created out of love of family and a lot of family togetherness!

I challenge you take the next 40 days and try a new meal every day. You may find some new favorites.

Starters and Beverages

Southern Sweet Tea

PREP TIME: 15 min
MAKES: 12 cups

There is an art to sweet tea, making sure that sugary goodness is completely blended into the tea. In case your nana didn't teach you, I'm sharing my mimi's recipe!

INGREDIENTS
- 8 cups water
- 1½ cup sugar
- 6 large tea bags
- Pinch of baking soda
- Fresh mint leaves
- Lemon wedges

EQUIPMENT
- Large pot

DIRECTIONS

1. Bring 8 cups of water to a boil. Add Sugar and continue boiling for 6 minutes.

2. Turn off heat and add pinch of baking soda and tea bags. Let steep for 5-7 minutes. Why baking soda? It helps neutralize the tanins that make tea a little bitter. you can leave it out if you prefer.

3. Remove tea bags and let cool. Add 4 cups cool water and stir.

4. Serve tea over ice with fresh mint sprigs or lemon slices.

What if it's not sweet enough?

If you have brewed the tea and find it not quite as sweet as your nana's, just create a simple syrup. It will incorporate easily into the tea. Simple syrup is 1/2 cup boiling water and 1/2 cup sugar - cook until dissolved.

Kathy's Fruit Tea

 PREP TIME
10 min

 MAKES
8 cups

One of my favorite summer drinks. It mixes the joy of sweet tea with all the freshness of citrus!

INGREDIENTS
Prepared warm Sweet Tea (recipe Page 6)
Frozen lemonade can
Frozen orange juice can
2 cinnamon sticks
5 whole cloves
Fresh mint leaves
Lemon slices
Orange slices

DIRECTIONS

1. Prepare 8 cups of sweet tea.

2. While tea is still warm, scoop ½ can of frozen orange juice and ⅓ can of frozen lemonade into tea. Stir until dissolved.

3. Add cinnamon and cloves and let spices steep for about 5 minutes.

4. Strain spices and serve over ice with mint and lemon or orange slices.

Want tea in the winter?

Great idea! Add pomegranate seeds to the warm tea with the citrus and allow too steep. Serve tea in a glass pitcher so everyone can enjoy the rich red berries.

Hot Spice Tea

 PREP TIME
5 min

 MAKES
8 cups

One of my favorite summer drinks. It mixes the joy of sweet tea with all the freshness of citrus!

INGREDIENTS
- 1 20oz container Instant orange drink
- 1 cup Instant powder tea
- ½ cup powdered lemonade
- 1 cup sugar
- 2 tablespoons cinnamon
- 1 teaspoon nutmeg

EQUIPMENT
- Air tight storage container 40oz

DIRECTIONS

1. Combine all ingredients and mix well.

2. Store in an airtight container.

3. When ready to make, bring water to a boil. Add 2-3 tablespoons of mix for each 8oz cup of water.

4. Mix well and enjoy!

Too hot for hot tea?

Try this tea served over ice for a spicy change of pace.

Dalgona Coffee

PREP TIME: 10 min
SERVES: 4

Dalgona coffee originated out of South Korea. The name refers to a type of Korean honeycomb toffee. It's delicious with an intense coffee taste.

INGREDIENTS
- 2 tablespoons instant coffee
- 2 tablespoons sugar
- 2 tablespoons water
- Milk
- Ice
- Cocoa powder or cinnamon (optional)

EQUIPMENT
- Hand Mixer/Whisk

DIRECTIONS

1. Mix together all three ingredients.

2. Using a hand mixer, beat until light in color and fluffy – similar to a meringue. You can use a whisk if you need an arm workout!

Putting it all together:

3. Fill a glass about 3/4 with Milk and Ice. Spoon the Coffee mixture on top to fill the cup. Sprinkle with cocoa powder or cinnamon if you like and serve. Use a straw or a spoon to mix coffee into milk before drinking.

Don't like it cold?

Try filling a coffee cup with 1/4 cup warmed milk, ½ brewed coffee and top with coffee mixture. Sprinkle with cocoa or cinnamon and serve

Back Porch Breeze

PREP TIME 10 min   **MAKES** 1 serving

This drink will bring back great memories made sitting on the back porch drinking a refreshing lemonade with friends and family--with a grown-up twist!

INGREDIENTS
- 2 ounces lemon vodka (chilled)
- ½ ounce triple sec
- 1 ounce lemon juice
- 1 ounce simple syrup
- 6 leaves basil
- 4 leaves mint plus garnish
- Lemon sugar
- 1 ounce lime sparkling water

DIRECTIONS

1. Muddle basil and mint leaves in a glass. Muddle means to press and bruise the herbs to release the flavors. You want to do it in your glass so all the good oils don't end up on your fingers! If you don't have a muddler, use the blunt end of a long handled tool. Press down and gently twist. Add simple syrup and let rest.

2. Into the syrup and leaves mixture, add the Vodka, Triple Sec and lemon juice. Shake well.

3. Rub edge of chilled glass with lemon and dip rim into lemon sugar. Add 3-4 ice cubes to glass. Strain Vodka mixture into glass. Add lime Perrier, quick stir and garnish with mint and lemon peel. Enjoy!

Back Porch Breeze
non-alcoholic

PREP TIME
10 min

MAKES
1 serving

This drink will bring back great memories made sitting on the back porch drinking a refreshing lemonade with friends and family!

INGREDIENTS

1 ounce lemon juice
3 ounces water
Juice of ½ orange (1 ounce)
1 ounce simple syrup
6 leaves basil
4 leaves mint plus garnish
Lemon sugar
1 ounce lime sparkling water

DIRECTIONS

1. Muddle basil and mint leaves in a glass. Muddle means to press and bruise the herbs to release the flavors. You want to do it in your glass so all the good oils don't end up on your fingers! If you don't have a muddler, use the blunt end of a long handled tool. Press down and gently twist. Add simple syrup and let rest.

2. Into the syrup and leaves mixture, add the orange juice, water and lemon juice. Shake well.

3. Rub edge of chilled glass with lemon and dip rim into lemon sugar. Add 3-4 ice cubes to glass. Strain Lemon mixture into glass. Add lime Perrier, quick stir and garnish with mint and lemon peel. Enjoy!

Cheese Board

PREP TIME	REST TIME	SERVES
15 min	15-60 min	4

Making a cheese plate for a small dinner party or large gathering can be intimidating. But actually, it's really simple once you learn how.

INGREDIENTS
(Suggestions in Directions)
- 3-5 Different cheeses
  - 1 hard cheese
  - 1 soft cheese
  - 1 semi-soft cheese
- Fresh fruit
- Nuts or dried fruit
- 1-2 spreads
- Bread or crackers

EQUIPMENT
- Platter (Cutting board, tray)
- Cheese knives
- Spreaders

DIRECTIONS

Cheese:

1. Select 3-5 different cheeses, depending on the size of your crowd. About 1-2 ounces per person. Remember – no flavored cheeses. You want the unique taste of each cheese to come through.

2. When picking the cheese, variety is the spice of life! So choose cheeses with distinct differences. Pick a soft cheese (e.g. camembert, goat, brie, gorgonzola), semi-soft (e.g. gouda, muster, harvarti) and hard cheese (e.g. Jarlsberg, gruyere, comté). Or pick cheese from different milk bases (e.g. goat's milk, cow's milk). Explore the cheeses, you might find a new favorite!

3. Set your harder cheeses out about one hour before serving. The softer cheeses won't need as much time. Allowing the cheese to come to room temperature will help all the flavors of the cheese come through.

4. Slice your firmer cheeses. This make it easier for people to eat and more likely they will enjoy. No one wants to fight with a hunk of cheese. If you have a rinded soft cheese, cut some of the rind off to make it easier for guests to gracefully cut a slice.

Bread:

5. Choose 1-2 Bread and/or Crackers. Choose a bread like a sliced baguette or crostini,

Cheese Board

multigrain crackers or parmesan crisps (see recipe page 21). Again, nothing too strong. You want to taste cheese not the bread.

Fruit:
6. Find a fresh fruit that is in-season to add to your platter. If you prefer, utilize dried fruit instead. In addition, add a small bowl of olives or cornichon pickles (you know, those tiny ones).

Nuts:
7. Include small nuts like almonds or cashews – being aware of your guests allergies.

Spreads:
8. Finally add one or two spreads. Do not put them on your cheeses. Let you guests explore the platter and make their own creations with the cornucopia you have provided.

Putting it all together:
9. First don't crowd the platter. Keep that in mind as you start to put things on the platter. Arrange your cheese around the center of your round platter. If you have a rectangular platter, lay them across the middle. Next, add any small bowls you have (olives, spreads, etc). Then lay the fruit and nuts onto the platter. Finally arrange the crackers or bread in the open spaces. Provide knives for cutting the cheeses as needed and spreaders for the spread. Now, you should have a beautiful cheese platter.

Charcuterie Board

PREP TIME	REST TIME	SERVES
15 min	15-60 min	4

A charcuterie board can be a beautiful array of colors and aromas! It's an abundant way to welcome guests or a delightful way to snack for dinner.

INGREDIENTS
(Suggestions in Directions)
- Cured meats
- Cheese
- Olives
- Nuts
- Fresh or dried fruit
- Crackers or baguette
- Thin breadsticks
- Jellies/Hummus/Honey

EQUIPMENT
- Board (cutting board, tray platter)
- Small ramekins
- Small/Med bowls
- A tall thin container
- Spreaders

DIRECTIONS

Meats:

1. This is the heart of the Charcuterie board so don't skimp here. Choose 3-5 different (depending on size of crowd). About 1-2 ounces person. Remember to pick different types and slice into different sizes. Prosciutto is always a favorite. Mix it up by wrapping it around pieces of fresh fruit. Slice it thinly. Hard salamis look great sliced and there are many varieties to choose from. Pepperoni can be cut into slices or chunks. Try going to your local meat shop and ask about some seasonal or favorite cuts of meat. They will cut the meats for you, too.

Cheese:

2. Plan on selecting 2-4 different cheeses, depending on the size of your crowd. About 1-2 ounces per person. Remember – no flavored cheeses. Just like the meat, have a variety to choose from. So, pick cheeses with distinct differences. There are soft cheeses (e.g. camembert, goat, brie, gorgonzola), semi-soft (e.g. gouda, muster, Havarti) and hard cheese (e.g. Jarlsberg, gruyere, comté). You can also pick cheese from different milk bases (e.g. goat's milk, cow's milk). Don't forget, you can buy pre-cubed or sliced cheese as well!

3. Set your harder cheeses out about one hour before serving. The softer cheeses won't need as much time. Allowing the cheese to come to room temperature will help all the flavors of the cheese come through.

Charcuterie Board

4. Slice your firmer cheeses. This make it easier for people to eat and more likely they will enjoy. No one wants to fight with a hunk of cheese. If you have a rinded soft cheese, cut some of the rind off to make it easier for guests to gracefully cut a slice.

Bread:
5. Place breadsticks in tall, thin container. Choose 1-2 additional breads and/or crackers. Something like a sliced baguette, crostini, or multigrain or buttery crackers. This tray can have an artistic or even fruited bread.

Fruit:
6. Find a fresh fruit that is in-season to add to your platter. Apricots are always a good complement to meats. If you prefer, utilize dried fruit instead. In addition, add a small bowl of olives or cornichon pickles (you know, those tiny ones). or other pickled vegetable. Roasted sweet peppers are great, too.

Nuts:
7. Include small nuts like almonds or cashews - being aware of your guests allergies.

Spreads:
8. Finally add one or two thinking about season and flavors of your meat/cheese. Brie begs for a jam or honey. Hummus is a nice option, be sure you have crackers. Bruschetta and flavored olive oils can be a good match with breads. Place them the ramekins or bowls.

Putting it all together.
9. Start with the meats! For variety, roll up, fold, or fan out the meat. Place different shapes and colors near each other to keep it visually interesting. Add in cheeses. Again, the goal is to have a plethora of colors and shapes. Place any small bowls you have, then lay the fruit and nuts onto the platter. Finally arrange the crackers/bread in the open spaces. Provide forks for meats, spreader, spoons for bowls and spreaders for the soft cheese. Now, you should have a beautiful charcuterie platter.

> **Seasonality?**
> Adapt your board to reflect the freshness of the seasons.
> Spring: light greens and pinks. (grapes, kiwis, radishes)
> Summer: rich Americana colors (peaches, blueberries, strawberries)
> Fall: autumn, pumpkin farm colors (pumpkin spread, spiced nuts, and apples.
> Winter: Christmas colors and scents (dried cranberries, rosemary, persimmons)

Balsamic Glaze

PREP TIME
10 min

COOK TIME
3 min

Balsamic vinegar adds great flavor to dishes, but this glaze adds a little extra depth of flavor and is thick enough to stay on.

INGREDIENTS

1 cup balsamic vinegar
¼ cup honey or molasses

EQUIPMENT

Saucepan
Storage container

DIRECTIONS

1. Combine vinegar and honey into a small saucepan. Heat over high heat. Once it begins to boil, reduce the heat to low and continue simmering to reduce the mixture by about two-thirds. It should easily coat the back of a spoon.

2. Remove from heat and cool. This can be stored in a sealed container for about one month.

Want more suggestions?

Use balsamic glaze on fresh grilled vegetables, grilled or bake chicken breasts or even on fresh berries.

Caprese Kabobs

PREP TIME 10 min   **MAKES** 12

Love caprese salad? This appetizer has all of flavor of caprese but in a finger food version.

INGREDIENTS
- 1 pint cherry/grape tomatoes
- 8 ounces small mozzarella balls
- 12 large basil leaves
- 12 skewers
- Salt and pepper
- 1 teaspoon olive oil
- 2 teaspoons balsamic glaze (recipe page 16)

DIRECTIONS

1. Drain and dry mozzarella balls. Wash and dry tomatoes and basil leaves.

2. Pierce the tomato all the way through with the skewer. Slide up about 1" from the top. Next, center a basil leaf on the skewer and push it up next to the tomato. If your leaf is too large, fold in half before putting on skewer. Finally pierce a mozzarella ball and push it up to basil. Repeat this pattern once more on this same skewer.

3. Continue assembling remaining skewers using this alternating pattern.

Putting it together:
4. Lay all skewers side by side on a platter. Sprinkle with salt and fresh ground pepper. Then drizzle with olive oil and balsamic glaze.

Looking for a twist?

Add color by using orange and red tomatoes.

Tortellini Skewers

PREP TIME 20 min MAKES 16-20

Tortellini skewers are filling appetizer with a light, refreshing flavor. It's espeically good in summer when the herbs and tomatoes are fresh off the vine.

INGREDIENTS
16 ounces cheese tortellini
½ cup olive oil
¼ cup red wine vinegar
2 cloves garlic, minced
1 shallot, roughly chopped
1 teaspoon basil
1 teaspoon oregano
¼ teaspoon salt
⅛ teaspoon black pepper
10 grape tomatoes, halved
Kosher salt and pepper
1 large red bell pepper
4 ounces fresh mozzarella,
35-40 small basil leaves

EQUIPMENT
Long toothpicks

Short on time?

Try using store-bought Italian dressing with some fresh herbs as a short cut.

DIRECTIONS
1. Cook the tortellini according to the package directions. Since it's fresh pasta, it won't take long. Drain when cooked.

2. Prepare peppers by cutting into ½ inch squares. Cube the cheese or use mozzarella balls.

3. Whisk together the 12 dressing ingredients. Add hot pasta to the dressing so flavors will be absorbed.

4. Let side until pasta is cooled. Then stir in the peppers, tomatoes and mozzarella.

5 Let this marinate up to overnight.

6. Using long toothpicks, assemble the appetizer by placing on the skewer in order tortellini, 1 basil leaf, pepper piece, mozzarella, basil, tomato, and tortellini.

Putting it together:
7. Finish putting all tortellini on skewers. Lay next to each other on a tray and drizzle with marinade, salt and pepper to taste.

Roasted Bruschetta

PREP TIME	OVEN TEMP	COOK TIME	SERVES
10 min	400F	10 min	6

This starter is quick, elegant and super easy. Always a winner when guests stop by.

INGREDIENTS
- 1 pint grape tomatoes
- 2 teaspoons olive oil
- 2 teaspoons minced garlic
- 8-10 basil leaves
- 1 tablespoon olive oil
- ½ teaspoon balsamic vinegar
- ½ teaspoon kosher salt
- ¼ teaspoon black pepper
- A pinch of red pepper
- A baguette loaf
- 1 garlic clove, halved

EQUIPMENT
- Cookie Sheet

DIRECTIONS

1. Pre Heat oven to 400 F.

2. Slice tomatoes in half and toss in 2 teaspoons olive oil. Spread on cookie sheet and roast in hot oven until soft and lightly browned, about 10 minutes. They should mush easily with a fork.

3. Meanwhile, slice basil leaves into thin strips. Mix basil with olive oil, balsamic vinegar, minced garlic, salt, pepper and red pepper. Set aside.

4. Slice Baguette into thin slices. Gently rub garlic cloves on bread face.

5. Toss roasted tomatoes while gently pressing on the tomatoes until thoroughly coated. Add more olive oil if needed.

Putting it together:

6. Place the tomato mixture into a bowl and place in the middle of a platter. Spread bread slices around the platter. Garnish as desired.

Not sure how to chop basil?

Gently stack the basil leaves together and roll up lengthwise. Slice the roll into thin slices, like slicing butter. Now you have thin strips called chiffonade!

Parmesan Crisps

PREP TIME	OVEN TEMP	COOK TIME	MAKES
5 min	400F	3 min	8-10 crisps

A quick way to dress up a salad or have as a delicious snack.

INGREDIENTS
½ Cup grated parmesan (about 2 ounces)
2 teaspoons oregano

EQUIPMENT
Cookie sheet

DIRECTIONS

1. Preheat the oven to 400 F. Line a cookie sheet with a silicone mat or parchment paper. Otherwise, the crisps will be difficult to get off the sheet.

2. Use pre-shredded cheese or grate about 2 ounces of parmesan using a box grater and mix with oregano.

3. Scoop about 2 inches of shredded cheese mixture onto baking sheet. Flatten out gently.

4. Bake at 400 F until golden and crisp, 3-5 minutes. Let it cool for about 5 minutes.

Putting it together:

5. Serve as a snack, as an addition for a salad or soup or serve with a dip.

Looking for variations?

Add one of the following:
½ teaspoon sea salt and 1 teaspoon coarsely ground black pepper
2 teaspoons rosemary or basil
½ teaspoon crushed red pepper
1 teaspoon dry minced onion
2 teaspoons garlic powder

> No one is born a great cook, one learns by doing.
>
> JULIA CHILD

Salads and Sides

Cucumber Carrot Salad

PREP TIME	REST TIME	MAKES
10 min	20 min	4 servings

Our garden produced an abundance of cucumbers this year. So this is one of the many ways we used them! It's refreshing with a slight Asian flavor. Works well for lunch or dinner.

INGREDIENTS
- 2 large cucumbers
- 1 cup carrots, matchsticks
- 2 tablespoons rice wine vinegar
- 1 tablespoons lime juice
- 2 tablespoons honey
- 1 tablespoon grape seed or olive oil
- ½ teaspoon sesame oil
- ½ teaspoon salt
- 1 tablespoon cilantro
- 1 tablespoon sesame seeds
- Red pepper flakes (optional)

DIRECTIONS
1. Thinly slice the cucumbers.

2. Mix together the vinegar, lime, honey, sesame, salt, cilantro and optional red pepper in a bowl.

3. Toss cucumbers and carrots into dressing.

4. Refrigerate for 20 minutes.

Putting it together:
5. Toss in sesame seeds and spoon into individual bowls.

For a dressier look, place cucumbers along outside edge and spoon carrot mixture into the center. Sprinkle with extra cilantro or sesame seeds if desired.

Want to make it a meal?

Add thinly sliced cooked chicken breast. Try sauting in a touch of sesame oil, salt, pepper and ginger.

Broccoli Slaw

PREP TIME: 10 min SERVES: 6

A wonderful healthy alternative to a regular salad!

INGREDIENTS

1 package broccoli slaw
1 pack chicken ramen noodles
1 tablespoons sesame seeds
2 tablespoons sliced almonds
1 teaspoon butter

Dressing:
½ cup salad oil
½ shallot minced (optional)
2 tablespoons cup sugar
2 tablespoons white wine vinegar
Seasoning packet from Ramen noodles

DIRECTIONS

1. In a salad bowl, pour in the broccoli slaw.

2. In a bowl, whisk together all ingredients for the dressing. Set aside.

3. Before opening ramen package, gently crush the noodles to break into small pieces. Heat a small saucepan over medium-low heat. Melt butter and add sesame seeds, almonds and ramen noodles. Continue sautéing until lightly browned. Remove from heat.

Putting it all together:
4. Sprinkle noodle mixture over slaw. Whisk dressing once more and pour just enough over slaw to coat lightly. Toss and serve.

Sherry Shallot Vinaigrette

PREP TIME: 10 min
MAKES: 5 oz

Light and tangy dressing, perfect for a summer salad!

INGREDIENTS

- 2 tablespoons sherry vinegar
- 1 tablespoon minced shallot
- ½ teaspoon Dijon mustard
- Salt and pepper to taste
- 6 tablespoons light olive oil
- Sugared almonds

DIRECTIONS

1. Combine the shallots and vinegar and if time allows, let sit for 10 minutes or all day if you prefer! This allows the shallots to soften and absorb some of the flavor. It really makes your dressing better.

2. Mix in Dijon mustard and drizzle in the olive oil. Combine well. Add a little salt and pepper to taste.

3. Top salad with sugared almonds.

Looking for Variations?

Add 3 tablespoons of your favorite chopped herbs for an even more summery taste.
Add a little bacon for a heartier taste.

Caprese Salad

PREP TIME 10 min   SERVES 4

This is the quintessential summer salad. It's refreshing, light and aromatic!

INGREDIENTS
- 3 large tomatoes
- 16 ounces fresh mozzarella
- 12 large basil leaves
- Salt and pepper
- 1 teaspoon olive oil
- 2 teaspoons balsamic glaze
  (recipe page 16)

EQUIPMENT
- Cookie sheet

DIRECTIONS
1. Thinly slice top and bottom off of each tomato then slice tomatoes into ¼-inch slices.

2. Slice the fresh mozzarella into ¼-inch round slices – try to have the same number of mozzarella slices as tomatoes.

Putting it together:
3. Pre-set salad by using four separate plates. Place one slice of mozzarella on the plate, then one basil leaf, topped with a tomato slice. Continue alternating with 3-4 slices of mozzarella, basil and tomato on a large platter. Sprinkle with salt and pepper, then drizzle with olive oil and balsamic glaze.

Looking for a twist?

Add color by using orange and red tomatoes. Add variety and vitamins by adding thinly slice cucumbers to the plate.

Remoulade Sauce

PREP TIME 10 min   MAKES 12 oz

Remoulade Sauce is traditionally French, but this is the Cajun version. It is basically a mayonnaise with some spces and a cajun flair! It's great on so many foods.

INGREDIENTS

- 1 cup mayonnaise
- 4 tablespoons Dijon mustard
- 1 tablespoon lemon juice
- 2 tablespoon chopped parsley
- 2 teaspoons capers, chopped
- ½ teaspoon hot sauce
- 1 teaspoon garlic, minced
- 1 shallot, minced
- 2 teaspoon Worcestershire sauce
- 2 teaspoons sweet paprika
- ¼ teaspoon kosher salt
- 1 teaspoon Cajun seasoning

DIRECTIONS

1. Whisk together all ingredients. Add additional hot sauce as needed.

2. Store in refrigerator. Even better if made in advance.

What to do with it?

Remoulade sauce is great on all kids of seafood.
Try it on
po' boy sandwiches, crab cakes or shrimp!

Rosemary Potatoes

PREP TIME	OVEN TEMP	COOK TIME	SERVES
10 min	500F	45 min	6

Another easy, flavorful side but plan ahead – this one takes about 45 minutes to cook.

INGREDIENTS

- 12-15 new potatoes
- 1 tablespoon olive oil
- 1 tablespoon rosemary
- 2 teaspoons kosher salt
- 1 teaspoon black pepper

EQUIPMENT

Cookie sheet

DIRECTIONS

1. Pre Heat oven to 425F. Line cookie sheet with foil.

2. Chop potatoes into quarters. Toss potatoes with olive oil, rosemary, salt and pepper.

3. Spread out on cookie sheet, single layer.

4. Cook for 45 min or until softened inside and crisp on the outside.

Putting it all Together:

5. Place potatoes in a bowl with a sprig of rosemary as garnish. Serve with chicken, pork or beef.

Want variations

Try using different herbs in place of rosemary to complement your main dish!

Mimi's Fried Okra

PREP TIME	COOK TIME	SERVES
10 min	15 min	6

Not an okra fan? Give this a try - my kids eat it like popcorn!

INGREDIENTS

- 1 pint okra
- 1 egg, beaten
- 1 package corn muffin mix
- 1 tablespoon vegetable oil

EQUIPMENT

- Cookie sheet

DIRECTIONS

1. Slice okra into ½ inch slices. For a thicker breading, soak in beaten egg for 5 min. Discard excess egg. Otherwise move on to step 2.

2. Add ½ box of muffin mix. Toss to coat.

3. Heat a large skillet over medium high heat. Add oil and heat. Add okra to hot pan in a single layer. Do in batches if you need to. Cook, browning on each side until crisp. Keep stirring so okra does not burn.

4. Remove from pan and place on paper towels to drain.

5. Serve while hot!

Want variations

Try using different herbs in place of rosemary to complement your main dish!

Sautéd Squash

PREP TIME	COOK TIME	SERVES
10 min	20 min	6

This is a really simple, dressed down, kid-friendly version of fried rice. But the flavor is great!

INGREDIENTS
- 2 yellow squash
- 1 zucchini squash
- 1 yellow onion
- ½ cup brown sugar
- 2 teaspoons vegetable oil

EQUIPMENT
- Skillet with lid

DIRECTIONS

1. Slice squash and zucchini into ½ inch slices. Discard the ends.

2. Heat skillet over medium heat. Add vegetable oil. When hot, add squash, onion and brown sugar.

3. Cover and cook for 12-15 min until squash is tender.

Want to a more caramelized finish?

Before removing from heat, add additional 1 tablespoon of brown sugar and stir to coat. Continue sauting squash with lid off for a few more minutes until sugar browns.

Sautéd Green Beans

PREP TIME 10 min   **COOK TIME** 20 min   **SERVES** 4

A delicious new way to serve up green beans. These are fancy enough you could call them Company Green Beans!

INGREDIENTS
12 ounces fresh green beans
1 tablespoon olive oil
1 teaspoon butter
1 red or yellow pepper
1 shallot, minced
1 teaspoon minced garlic
1 lemon
Salt and pepper

EQUIPMENT
Large pot
Skillet

DIRECTIONS

1. Cut pepper into long thin strips. Set aside. Trim ends off green beans. Fill pot 3/4 with water and bring to a boil.

2. Blanch green beans by placing them in boiling water to cook for 3-5 minutes – just until tender. You do not want floppy beans! Drain out the hot water and soak beans in cool water to stop the cooking. Then drain.

3. Heat a large skillet over medium high heat. Add oil and butter. When melted add peppers and cook 3-4 minutes. Add garlic. Cook just until the garlic starts to brown. You will begin to smell the garlic. Lower the heat to medium and mix in green beans, zest of lemon and juice from 1/2 lemon.

4. Continue to toss with peppers until beans are heated again. Salt and pepper to taste.

Don't have fresh beans?

Keep frozen beans on hand. Let them thaw. Then skip the blanching step!

Granny's Green Beans

PREP TIME	COOK TIME	SERVES
10 min	2 hours	8

Best green beans you'll ever eat. If you had a southern granny, you know what I'm talking about!

INGREDIENTS

- 2 large cans Italian flat green beans
- 8 slices bacon
- 2 teaspoons salt
- 1 teaspoon pepper
- ½ teaspoon garlic powder
- 1 small yellow onion
- 4 cups chicken stock

EQUIPMENT

- Large pot
- Skillet

DIRECTIONS

1. Cook bacon in microwave or stove until slightly cooked. Chop into pieces.

2. Dice onion into small pieces.

3. Drain the can of beans and put them in the pot. Add bacon, salt pepper and onion to the pot with the chicken stock. Be sure beans are covered.

4. Cook for about 2 hours on low heat or 4-5 hours in a crock pot. Salt and pepper to taste.

5. Place a large pat of butter on top of beans prior to serving.

No Flat green beans?

No problem! Substitute fresh or frozen snap beans.

Balsamic Asparagus

PREP TIME	OVEN TEMP	COOK TIME	SERVES
5 min	450F	9 min	4

Asparagus is a great side dish with many dishes including fish, chicken and beef. It works well with subtle flavors as well as strong flavors.

INGREDIENTS

1 bundle of asparagus
1 pint cherry tomatoes, halved
1 teaspoon olive oil
3 tablespoons balsamic vinegar
¼ cup parmesan cheese
½ kosher salt
¼ teaspoon black pepper

EQUIPMENT

Cookie Sheet

DIRECTIONS

1. Line cookie sheet with foil.

2. Remove tough ends from asparagus. Drizzle olive oil, salt and pepper on asparagus and toss to coat.

3. Spread asparagus on cookie sheet and sprinkle cheese over asparagus.

4. Cook until tender, 5-7 minutes.

5. Put vinegar in a saucepan and cook over medium heat until reduced.

6. Remove from oven.

Putting it together:
7. Arrange asparagus on a platter. Zest lemon onto asparagus. Serve hot.

Looking for a twist?

Try wrapping a slice of prosciutto around 3-4 stalks of asparagus prior to baking.

Lemon Roasted Asparagus

PREP TIME	OVEN TEMP	COOK TIME	SERVES
5 min	450F	9 min	4

Asparagus pairs well with many different flavors. This recipe in particular is refreshing and pairs well with summer!

INGREDIENTS
- 1 bundle of asparagus
- 1½ teaspoon minced garlic
- 1 tablespoon olive oil
- 2 Lemons
- ½ teaspoon kosher salt
- ¼ teaspoon black pepper

EQUIPMENT
Cookie Sheet

DIRECTIONS
1. Line cookie sheet with foil.

2. Remove tough ends from asparagus. Drizzle olive oil, juice from 1 lemon and garlic on asparagus and toss to coat. Add salt and pepper.

3. Spread asparagus on cookie sheet. Thinly slice remaining lemon and lay on asparagus.

4. Cook until tender, 5-7 minutes.

5. Remove from oven.

Putting it together:

6. Arrange asparagus on a platter. Zest lemon onto asparagus. Serve hot.

Looking for variety?

Try slicing red and yellow peppers into spears and cook along side the asparagus.

Roasted Root Vegetables

PREP TIME	OVEN TEMP	COOK TIME	SERVES
15 min	375F	20 min	4

While root vegetables bring up visions of fall, search the stores for what's in season and substitute them in so you can enjoy this year round.

INGREDIENTS
- 2 large carrots
- 10-12 red potatoes
- 1 red onion
- 1 butternut squash
- 1 parsnip
- 1 tablespoon olive oil
- 1 teaspoon thyme
- ½ teaspoon salt
- ⅛ teaspoon pepper
- Balsamic Glaze (optional- recipe page 16)

EQUIPMENT
Cookie sheet

DIRECTIONS

1. Chop vegetables. Potatoes should be quartered. Onion should be cut in half and then sliced into 1 ½ inch slices. The parsnip and carrots should be peeled sliced in half length wise and then sliced into ½-inch moon shapes. The butternut squash should be peeled sliced into 1-inch cubes.

2. Toss all vegetables with olive oil, sprinkled with thyme, salt and pepper.

3. Spread out on foil lined cookie sheet. Make sure there is space the vegetables roast and not steam. Put on two cookie sheets if needed.

4. Cook in 375F oven for about 15-20 minutes, until vegetables are tender.

5. If desired, drizzle with balsamic glaze immediately before serving.

Looking for a little sweet?

Add a teaspoon of melted chocolate to 2 tablespoons balsamic glaze to dress up your veggies.

Oven-Roasted Broccoli

PREP TIME	OVEN TEMP	COOK TIME	SERVES
5 min	375F	5-7 min	4

Give broccoli a make-over with this garlic seasoned oven-roasted broccoli recipe.

INGREDIENTS
- 3 stalks of broccoli
- 1 tablespoon oil
- ¾ teaspoon salt
- ¾ teaspoon minced garlic
- ½ teaspoon garlic powder
- ¼ teaspoon pepper

EQUIPMENT
- Cookie Sheet

DIRECTIONS
1. Line cookie sheet with foil.

2. Slice broccoli tops off of main stalk, leaving just a little stalk on each. Toss broccoli with olive oil. Mix in salt, garlic and pepper.

3. Spread on cookie sheet. Bake in 375F oven for 5-7 minutes – until broccoli is tender and starts to brown.

4. Serve while warm.

Looking for more flavor?

Cut back on the garlic and add minced ginger instead!
Be sure to cook broccoli till crisp - the crunch makes it fun.

Bacon Brussel Sprouts

PREP TIME 10 min | **OVEN TEMP** Broil | **COOK TIME** 25 min | **SERVES** 6

Brussel Sprouts can be tough to love. But these thinly sliced, bacon flavored sprouts are delightful!

INGREDIENTS

- 4 strips bacon
- 1 small shallot, thinly sliced
- 1 clove garlic, minced
- 1 bag brussel sprouts thin sliced
- ½ teaspoon salt
- ½ teaspoon black pepper
- 1 teaspoon bourbon (optional)
- 1 tablespoon honey

EQUIPMENT

- Skillet
- Cookie sheet

DIRECTIONS

1. Cut off ends of brussel sprouts and peel off any yellow outside leaves. Slice into thin slices.

2. Cook bacon in skillet until just cooked not crispy. Chop bacon. Leave bacon grease in skillet.

3. Increase heat to medium-high heat. Add brussels sprouts, shallot and garlic to the skillet. Sauté until brussels sprouts are bright green, about 3-5 minutes.

4. Add salt, pepper, bourbon, honey, and bacon. Stir to coat, then transfer to cookie sheet.

5. Broil 1-2 minutes, or until brussels sprouts are crispy. Watch carefully so that they do not burn.

6. Remove from oven and serve immediately.

Fried Rice

PREP TIME 10 min **COOK TIME** 20 min **SERVES** 6

This is a really simple, dressed down, kid-friendly version of fried rice. But the flavor is great!

INGREDIENTS
- 4 cups white rice, prepared
- 2 eggs, lightly beaten
- 3 tablespoons vegetable oil
- ½ teaspoon sesame oil
- 1 teaspoon salt
- 1 teaspoon minced ginger
- 1 cup peas and carrots
- 2 tablespoons green onions, diced
- 1 tablespoon oyster sauce (Hoisin or soy as substitutes)
- 1 tablespoon Soy sauce

EQUIPMENT
- Wok or large pan

DIRECTIONS

1. Heat wok over medium high heat. Add 1 tablespoon oil. Add eggs and scramble. Set aside.

2. To wok, add another tablespoon of vegetable oil and sesame oil. Add cooked rice. Cook 4-5 minutes, stirring, to evaporate moisture, infuse flavor.

3. To the rice, add salt, ginger, peas, carrots and onions. Continue cooking for 3 minutes.

Putting it together:

4. Finally, add the oyster sauce and soy sauce to the wok and combine well. Serve while hot.

Want to make it a meal?

Small dice your favorite protein (chicken, pork, beef). Cook thoroughly. Better yet, use left overs. Then add the cooked protein to the rice when you add in the vegetables.

> People want honest, flavourful food, not some show-off meal that takes days to prepare.
>
> Ted Allen

Breads

Dinner Biscuits

PREP TIME	OVEN TEMP	RISE TIME	COOK TIME	MAKES
15 min	400F	75 min	20 min	15

Buttery, flaky, hearty biscuits that will stand up to dinner! These take a little longer because they have yeast.

INGREDIENTS
- 1 tablespoon sugar
- ¼ cup warm water (90-110F)
- 1 tablespoon active dry yeast
- 4½+ cups all-purpose flour
- 2 teaspoons baking powder
- 1½ teaspoon baking soda
- 1 teaspoon kosher salt
- 3 tablespoon sugar
- 2 cups chilled buttermilk
- ¼ cup shortening, cold
- 1 stick butter chilled plus more melted for brushing

EQUIPMENT
- Cookie Sheet
- 2"-3" cookie cutter

DIRECTIONS

1. Combine water, 1 tablespoon sugar and yeast in a bowl and let stand for 5 minutes - should be frothy.

2. In a separate bowl, stir together remaining dry ingredients.

3. Using a box grater and the large holes, grate the butter into the dry ingredients. Mix with your hands just as needed to incorporate and break down a little more.

4. Fold the yeast mixture and buttermilk into the dry mixture. Keep stirring until it forms a ball. Turn out dough onto floured surface. Knead the dough by pressing it out and folding it on itself. Do this 8 or 10 times. The dough will become smooth. Form into a ball and place in a bowl. Cover with a cloth and place in a warm, draft-free place to rise. Let rise for 1 hour.

5. Pre-heat oven to 400F. Turn dough back out on to floured surface. Roll the dough out to about 1/2-1 inch thick. Then fold it in half and in half again. Repeat this process 1-2 more times. You are building layers into your biscuits, but don't get excited and do this a bunch of times! You will over work your dough.

6. On the final roll out, roll dough to 1 inch thick. Using a 3" circle cutter, cut biscuits and place on cookie sheet next to each other. Place in freezer for 15 minutes if you have time. Brush the tops with melted butter.

7. Bake on 400F until golden brown, 18 to 22 minutes, depending on size. If they start to get too brown, tent with aluminum foil until the insides are cooked.

8. Brush again with melted butter and serve warm.

Granny's Biscuits

PREP TIME	OVEN TEMP	COOK TIME	MAKES
15 min	450F	10 min	16 biscuits

These biscuits are a taste of home. Light and fluffy, perfect with honey, eggs and bacon. And best of all, they are fast.

INGREDIENTS
- 2 cups self-rising flour
- 1 teaspoon baking soda (optional)
- 1 stick cold butter
- ¾ cup-1 cup cold buttermilk
- 2 tablespoons melted butter

EQUIPMENT
Cookie Sheet

DIRECTIONS

1. Put flour in a bowl. Mix in baking soda if using. I know self-rising flour has leavening in it, but I like to ensure a little extra rise.

2. Using a box grater, grate in the butter. Cut it together until crumbly. Do not overwork into a dough.

3. Stir in the buttermilk to create a non-sticky dough.

4. Roll out onto a lightly floured surface. Fold the dough back onto itself and roll out again to about 1/2"-1" depending on how tall you like your biscuits! Using a 2" cutter, cut out biscuits and lay on cookie sheet with edges touching.

5. Place cookie sheet in freezer for about 10 minutes. Then brush with melted butter and place directly into 450F oven. Bake about 10 minutes, until golden brown.

Rosemary Bread

PREP TIME	OVEN TEMP	RISE TIME	COOK TIME
15 min	400F	20 min	20 min

Quick, warm and flavorful! This recipe will make you bread baker.

INGREDIENTS
- 1½ cups warm water
- 1 tablespoons honey
- 1 teaspoon salt
- 1 tablespoon active dry yeast (about 2 packets)
- 2 teaspoons rosemary
- 4-4½ cups all-purpose flour
- 2 teaspoons butter, melted
- Kosher salt
- Garlic powder

EQUIPMENT
- Mixer with bread hook
- Cookie Sheet

DIRECTIONS

1. Combine the water, honey, salt and yeast in mixing bowl. Let sit for 5 minutes, you'll see foamy bubbles. This means the yeast is blooming! If you don't see bubbles your yeast may be old or maybe your water was too hot/cold. Try again.

2. Add rosemary and 4 cups flour. Mix until dough no longer sticky, probably 2-3 minutes. Touch it! Is it stuck to your fingers or just sticky? If it stuck to your fingers, add 1/4 cup flour and turn the mixer on again. Do this until dough is sticky but not clinging to your fingers. If you add too much flour add a little water.

3. Remove dough from mixer and form the dough into a round loaf. Place on a parchment lined cookie sheet and cover with a towel. Let sit on the counter or in a cold oven for 20-30 minutes. It will grow larger but will not double like regular bread recipes.

4. Heat oven to 400F. Brush dough with melted butter and sprinkle with Kosher salt and garlic powder. Cut three slits diagonally in the top of the dough and bake for 16-20 mins.

Need Substitutions?

Out of AP Flour? Try Bread Flour!
Have Fresh rosemary? Use about 1 Tablespoon.
No rosemary? Try oregano.

Cinnamon Challah Bread

PREP TIME	OVEN TEMP	RISE TIME	COOK TIME	MAKES
15 min	325F	2 hours	30 min	1 loaf

This bread is delicious, sweet and delicate. It will be your go-to breead for breakfast or for a sweet treat.

INGREDIENTS

- 1¼ cup warm water
- 1 packet instant yeast
- 1 teaspoon sugar
- 4 to 5 cups flour
- ¼ cup sugar or honey
- 2 teaspoons salt
- 1 tablespoon cinnamon
- 2 eggs
- 1 egg yolk (keep egg white)
- 3 tablespoons canola oil
- 3 tablespoons brown sugar
- 1 tablespoon cinnamon
- ½ teaspoon nutmeg

EQUIPMENT

- Mixer with bread hook
- Cookie Sheet

DIRECTIONS

1. In a small bowl stir yeast, with water and 1 teaspoon sugar. Let rest for 5 minutes until it has become foamy.

2. In a mixing bowl, combine 4 C. of flour, sugar, salt & 1 tablespoon cinnamon. With a dough hook attached, add the eggs, yolk and oil (and honey if using). It will become a rough or shaggy dough.

3. Next, add yeast mixture to flour mixture. Continue kneading in mixer for 7 minutes. Add a little flour if dough continues to be too sticky. You want it to be able hold it's shape.

4. Form the dough into a soft, smooth ball. Place in a greased bowl and let rise for 1 hour or until doubled.

5. Combine Brown sugar, cinnamon and nutmeg in a bowl. Set aside.

6. Punch down dough and divide into 3 equal pieces. Roll out each piece into 15 x 4 inch rectangle. Place some of the brown sugar mixture along the vertical middle of each rectangle. Pinch the side together, forming a rope-shaped dough 15 inches long. Gently roll it to seal the rope. Repeat with the remain rectangles.

7. Braid the dough. To do this, place the stands next to each other. Starting in the middle, begin braiding to one end. Tuck the ends under. Starting in the middle again braid to the other end and tuck those ends under.

8. Place braided loaf on parchment lined cookie sheet. Let rise 1 hour.

9. Beat reserved egg white with 1 tablespoon water. Brush egg white mixture on loaf, coating completely. Bake in 325F oven for 30 minutes.

Dinner Rolls

PREP TIME	OVEN TEMP	RISE TIME	COOK TIME	MAKES
15 min	325F	40 min	20 min	16 rolls

This rolls can be made small and used as dinner rolls, but they are hearty enough to make a little bigger and use for sandwiches.

INGREDIENTS

1 cups milk, warm (105-115F)
1 tablespoon active dry yeast
2 tablespoons sugar, divided
2 tablespoons melted butter
½ cup water
2 teaspoons salt
5 cups flour
1 egg, for brushing on top

EQUIPMENT

Mixer with bread hook
Cookie Sheet

DIRECTIONS

1. Mix milk, yeast, butter and sugar together. Let stand for 5 minutes while the yeast blooms, or gets frothy.

2. Add in water, 4 cups flour and salt. Add additional flour ¼ cup at a time until a smooth dough forms.

3. Form dough into a ball and place in a greased bowl. Cover and let rise for 20 minutes.

4. Punch dough down and divide dough into 16 equal parts. Roll each into a ball. Don't work the dough. Place on cookie sheet next to each other. Cover and let rise for another 20 minutes.

5. Beat one egg and brush gently on top of the rolls. Bake in a 325F oven for 20 minutes or until golden brown.

French Bread
(under two hours)

PREP TIME	OVEN TEMP	RISE TIME	COOK TIME	MAKES
15 min	375F	90 min	20 min	2 loaves

French bread in under two hours? Yes indeed! This is as close as you can get to that delicious, crusty-chewy bread without spending 30 hours preparing! Give it a try!

INGREDIENTS
- 4 cups all purpose flour
- 1 tablespoon active dry yeast
- 1 teaspoon salt
- 1 tablespoon sugar
- 1¾ cups warm water 110F
- 1 egg white, beaten
- 1 tablespoon water

EQUIPMENT
- Mixer with bread hook
- Cookie Sheet
- Metal pan

DIRECTIONS

1. Mix water, yeast and sugar together in a bowl. Let stand for 5 minutes while the yeast blooms, or gets frothy.

2. Add in 4 cups flour and salt mix until flour completely incorporated. Mix another 7 minutes at medium speed. Alternatively, you can knead by hand for 10 minutes.

3. Form dough into a ball and place in a greased bowl. Cover and let rise for about 1 hour. It will have doubled.

4. Spray cookie sheet with cooking spray, line with parchment or sprinkle with cornmeal.

5. Punch dough down and divide dough into half. Roll one half out into a large rectangle, about 15x10. The size of a small cookie sheet. Take the long size and begin rolling the dough up on itself. Place the roll on the cookie sheet seam side down. Tuck the ends under to make a "neat" roll. Repeat with remaining half of dough.

6. Beat egg with 1 tablespoon water and brush gently on top of the bread. Cut 3-4 slits in the top of each loaf. Cover and let rise for another 30 minutes.

7. Pre heat oven to 375F. Place metal pan in oven. It really does need to be metal so it does not crack. Pour about ½ of water into pan - be careful of the steam. Place cookie sheet on rack above water pan and bake for 20-25 minutes or until golden brown.

> Laughter is brightest in the place where the food is.
>
> Irish Proverb

Main Dishes

Orange Chicken

PREP TIME	COOK TIME	SERVES
15 min	20 min	6

One of our favorite last minute meals! Even my kids' friends request this chicken. It will become one of your favorties, too.

INGREDIENTS
- 4 boneless chicken breasts
- ¾ cup flour (any kind)
- 1 teaspoon ground ginger
- ½ teaspoon salt
- ¼ teaspoon pepper
- ½ teaspoon garlic
- 2 teaspoons olive oil
- 1 cup white wine
- 2 tablespoons orange
- ½ cup orange marmalade
- orange zest
- Salt and pepper
- Parsley and orange slices

EQUIPMENT
- Large skillet

DIRECTIONS

1. Slice each piece of chicken to make thinner using a butterfly technique. Starting at the thicker end, slice into the side of the chicken moving towards the thin point. Be sure to cut all way through. This creates a thinner and more even piece of meat. Use a meat pounder to gently even out the thickness if necessary.

2. Combine flour, ginger, salt and pepper in a shallow dish. Lightly dredge (meaning turn in the flour to coat all sides) each piece of chicken through the flour.

3. Sauté chicken. Heat a large pan over medium heat. Add 1-2 teaspoons olive oil and heat for 1 minute. Cook chicken in batches (3-4 at a time) until lightly browned on each side. Chicken should be 180F and not pink. Set cooked chicken on plate and cover to keep warm.

4. In the same hot pan, gently add wine and lemon juice to deglaze pan. Increase heat, scraping bottom of pan. Continue to boil until the liquid is reduced by half. Add the orange marmalade and orange zest. Once incorporated, add the chicken back to the pan, making sure it is coated with sauce and cook for 1-2 minutes.

Putting it all together:
5. Arrange on a platter and with orange slices and sprinkle with parsley.

Don't want to fry?

Try baking the chicken on a lightly greased cookie sheet for 10 min at 375F. Then broil each side for about 1-2 min, just until crispy. But don't walk away-once they start to brown they will burn quickly!

Puff Pastry Chicken

PREP TIME	OVEN TEMP	COOK TIME	SERVES
15 min	375F	25 min	6

I make this recipe without any cheese since one of my tribe does not like cheese. Amazing, right? But you could easily add some parmesan into the puff pastry or use an herbed cheese spread.

INGREDIENTS
- 1 package thawed puff pastry
- 3 chicken breasts
- Italian dressing
- 2 tablespoons butter, melted
- Salt and pepper

EQUIPMENT
- Cookie sheet

DIRECTIONS

1. Cut the chicken breasts in half length-wise to thin them and then cut in half across. Salt and pepper lightly.

2. Unfold the thawed puff pastry. Give it a little stretch in both directions. Cut into 6 equal squares.

3. On each square place a piece of chicken.

4. Working quickly, add about 1teaspoon of Italian Dressing on top of the chicken then bring each of the 4 corners together in the center and pinch together. It should look like little envelopes. Pinch along the seams to close tightly. Continue with the remaining pieces.

5. Place apart on cookie sheet and brush each with melted butter.

Putting it all together:

6. Bake 375F for 15-20 minutes. Be sure chicken is fully cooked

---

Looking for substitutes?

Substitute Herbed cheese spread or Honey Mustard dressing instead of Italian Dressing

Italian Chicken Pasta

PREP TIME	COOK TIME	SERVES
15 min	30 min	6

This is a great all in one meal that can be on your table in 45 minutes! Something for everyone, including cheese and bacon!

INGREDIENTS

- ¼ box of fettuccine
- ½ tablespoon salt
- ½ tablespoon olive oil
- 8 slices bacon
- 1 pound chicken breast
- 2 cloves garlic, minced
- 6-8 grape tomatoes, halved
- 1 cup heavy cream
- ½ cup chicken broth
- 1 teaspoon Italian seasoning
- ½ teaspoon red pepper
- 5 ounces baby spinach
- ¾ cup grated Parmesan (optional)
- Lemon zest
- 3 tablespoons fresh basil
- Salt and Pepper

DIRECTIONS

1. Cook Pasta: Add ½ tablespoon of salt, ½ tablespoon olive oil to water in a large pot and bring to boil. Add fettuccine and cook until al dente – about 9-11 minutes; drain.

2. While the pasta is cooking, place the bacon in a large skillet. Cook over medium-high heat, until crispy about 7-9 minutes.

3. Reserve the oil in the skillet by removing the bacon with a fork and place on paper towel lined plate to drain.

4. Cut the chicken into 1' pieces. Lightly salt and pepper and add to the medium high skillet with the bacon grease – careful not to crowd or the chicken will steam. Cook until no longer pink, about 6 minutes. Transfer to the plate with the bacon.

Putting it together:

5. Have all remaining ingredients ready to add to skillet. Place the skillet you just cooked the chicken in over medium heat. Add garlic, tomatoes, Italian seasoning, red pepper, broth and cream. Bring to a simmer. It will reduce slightly and thicken. Add the spinach and allow it to begin to wilt. Quickly add the bacon and chicken, tossing in the sauce. Finally, mix in fettuccine and parmesan and toss again until pasta well coated; season to taste with salt and pepper. Top with lemon zest and basil and serve hot.

Traditional Beef Stew

PREP TIME 20 min   **COOK TIME** 2 hours   **SERVES** 6

Beef stew is the perfect comfort food. You can slow cook this all day in a crock pot or whip it up in a couple of hours. You'll love the rich, complex flavors in this recipe.

INGREDIENTS

- ¼ cup all-purpose flour
- ½ teaspoon freshly pepper
- 1 pound beef stewing meat
- 2 tablespoons red wine vinegar
- 1 cup red wine
- 3 cups beef broth or water
- ⅓ cup tomato paste
- ½ teaspoon salt
- 2 teaspoons minced garlic
- 2 bay leaves
- 1 medium onion 1 inch diced
- 2 stalks celery ½ inch diced
- 12-15 baby carrots
- 1 pound new potatoes, halved
- Vegetable Oil

EQUIPMENT

Dutch Oven/Large Pot

DIRECTIONS

1. Cut beef into 1" cubes. Mix the flour and pepper in a plastic bag, then add the beef and shake well. Shake off excess. Heat a Dutch oven or large pot over medium high heat. When edge is hot to touch, add about 1 tablespoon of oil. Wait 1 minute to heat oil.

2. Cooking in batches, gently place beef into pot; do not overcrowd. Turn the beef so it browns on all sides. Remove from pot and set aside.

3. In the same pot, add the vinegar and wine and scrape the bottom of pot to deglaze.

4. Return the beef to the pot with the wine mixture and add tomato paste, garlic, salt, bay leaves, vegetables and water/beef broth. Bring mixture to a boil then reduce to a simmer. Cover and cook until beef is tender about 1 1/2 - 2 hours depending on size of meat and vegetables.

5. Keep an eye on the water level – add water/broth as needed.

Putting it together:

6. Simply season with salt and pepper and serve in a bowl. Garnish with parsley and serve with good crusty bread (check out the bread recipes starting on page 41).

Want to save for later?

Consider throwing in some peas right before serving for a little extra color and vitamins! If you want freeze for a later date, skip the potatoes and add when you are ready to eat.

Grandma's Beef Chili

PREP TIME 15 min | **COOK TIME** 20 min | **SERVES** 8

This recipe can be made pretty quickly in a pinch and it's always a winner! Not too spicy, not sweet and loaded with meat.

INGREDIENTS
- 3 lbs. of ground beef
- 1 large white onion, minced
- 1 large 32oz can tomato juice
- 1 packet chili spice mix
- 2 large cans mild chili beans
- 3/4 teaspoon red pepper
- ⅓ cup sugar
- Pinch of cinnamon
- 1 teaspoon salt
- ½ teaspoon pepper

EQUIPMENT
- Crock Pot/Large pot
- Skillet

DIRECTIONS

1. Brown ground beef, chopped onion, salt and pepper in large skillet. Drain excess fat.

2. In a large pot or slow cooker, mix together the tomato juice, chili mix, beans, and remaining spices. Then add cooked meat and onions, stir well. Simmer until well heated.

Putting it all together:

3. Serve with shredded Cheddar Cheese, sour cream, chopped green onions and oyster crackers.

Have some time?

This chili is even better if you let is slow simmer a couple hours before serving, and if possible, refrigerate overnight!

American Tacos

PREP TIME	COOK TIME	SERVES
5 min	15 min	6

Definitely an Americanized version of taco, but mild enough to be loved by kids of all ages.

INGREDIENTS
- 2 lb. ground beef
- 2 tablespoons taco mix (below)
- ½ cup water
- Fixings of your choice

EQUIPMENT
Skillet

DIRECTIONS
1. Brown ground beef in a skillet over medium high heat. Drain off excess fat.

2. Add 2 tablespoons of Taco Mix and water and simmer for 10 minutes. Keep an eye on the water levels. You want it dry with a slight crunch but not dried out.

Putting it together:

3. Put together a do-it-yourself taco bar. Include hard and soft shells, shredded cheese, salsa, beans sour cream, guacamole, cilanto and lime.

TACO MIX

INGREDIENTS
- 4 teaspoon chili powder
- 2 teaspoons ground cumin
- 2 teaspoons corn starch (optional but helps with coating and crunch)
- 1 teaspoon black pepper
- 1 teaspoon smoked paprika
- ½ teaspoon garlic powder
- ½ teaspoon onion powder
- ½ teaspoon sea salt
- ½ teaspoon dried oregano
- ¼ teaspoon crushed red pepper flakes (or more)

DIRECTIONS
Mix all dry ingredients in a bowl. Store extra in an airtight container.

This spice mix is great for tacos, burritos, beef, chicken or pork!

Makes 4 tablespoons.

Picante Chicken

PREP TIME	COOK TIME	SERVES
10 min	25 min	6

Delicious, one pan meal ready in almost 30 minutes!

INGREDIENTS
½ medium onion, small dice
½ green pepper, small dice
2 teaspoons minced garlic
1¾-2 cups chicken broth
1 jar salsa
1 cup rice, uncooked
6 skinless chicken breasts
1 tablespoon cilantro
Vegetable oil, for frying
Salt and pepper

Toppings:
Avocado peeled and sliced
Tomato chopped
Cheddar or Jack Cheese
Sour cream
Cilantro

EQUIPMENT
Skillet with lid

DIRECTIONS

1. In a large skillet that has a lid, heat 1 tablespoon of oil. Add onions and garlic for about 2 minutes but don't let the garlic brown.

2. Add the chicken broth, cilantro and salsa. Bring to a boil and then add the rice and stir and bring to a simmer.

3. Lightly salt and pepper the chicken and lay in the bed of rice. Push down slightly.

4. Cover the pot and continue simmering for 15-20 minutes to cook the chicken. Keep an eye on the water level or the rice and chicken will burn to the bottom of the pan. Add about ¼ cup of water as needed.

5. Remove from heat and let stand. The rice will re-absorb some of the remaining liquid.

Putting it together:
6. Sprinkle a little cilantro over the dish to add color and flavor. Serve the chicken salsa dish with the toppings on the side.

Know what people like

Try plating each meal, layering chicken and rice then cheese, tomatoes, sour cream, sprinkle with cilantro and add avocado slices on the side.

Chicken Tortilla Soup

PREP TIME	COOK TIME	SERVES
20 min	1 hour	6-8

This soup gets its rich flavor from creating a roux and adding heavy whipping cream. You'll be licking the bowl!

INGREDIENTS

- ¼ cup butter
- ½ cup vegetable oil
- ¾ cup flour
- 2 lb chicken deboned
- 1 large onion chopped
- 2 carrots diced
- 4 ribs of celery diced
- 4 cloves garlic, minced
- 8 cups chicken broth
- 1 teaspoon cumin
- 1 teaspoon chili powder
- 1 teaspoon salt
- 1 teaspoon lemon pepper
- 2 tablespoons Steak Sauce
- 4 oz tomato paste
- ¼ cup whipping cream
- 2 tablespoons cornstarch
- ½ cup Monterey Jack cheese
- 1½ teaspoon cilantro
- 1 teaspoon lime juice
- Tortilla strips or chips
- Diced avocados
- Sour cream
- Cilantro
- Lime wedges
- Monterey Jack Cheese

DIRECTIONS

1. In a skillet over high heat, add 1 tablespoon of oil and sear all sides of chicken and set aside.

2. Add remaining oil and flour to pan. Make a light colored roux by cooking the oil and flour until light brown, scrapping the bottom of the pan to get particles, 10 minutes.

3. Add onions, carrots, celery to roux and sauté until onions soften. Add garlic. Place chicken and roux/vegetable mixture into large pot. Add chicken broth, cumin, chili powder, salt, pepper, tomato paste and steak sauce and bring to boil. Reduce heat and simmer for 30-45 min.

4. Remove chicken. Shred and then replace in pot.

5. Mix well in a separate bowl-cornstarch and heavy whipping cream. Don't skip this or you will end up with chunks of cornstarch. Diluting the cornstarch with the whipping cream allows the cornstarch to be mixed into the soup. Add to the soup and stir well.

Putting it together:

6. Add 1/2 cup cheese, cilantro and lime and serve. Serve soup with all of the toppings in separate bowls so each person can create their own version.

Chicken Creole & Grits

PREP TIME	COOK TIME	SERVES
30 min	20 min	4

"Creole" refers to the French and Spanish settlers in New Orleans. The food is an amazing blend of flavors: German, Spanish, French, African, and more.

INGREDIENTS
- 1 cup flour
- ½ cup vegetable oil plus 2 additional tablespoons
- ½ yellow onion chopped
- 1 green bell pepper
- 2 cloves of garlic, minced
- 1¼ cup chicken broth
- 6 oz tomato paste
- 1 can diced tomatoes
- 1 teaspoon paprika
- 1 teaspoon thyme
- ½ teaspoon oregano
- 3 bay leaves
- ½ cup flour (additional)
- 1 teaspoon garlic salt
- 1 teaspoon ground red pepper
- 1 teaspoon oregano
- 1 teaspoon black pepper
- ½ teaspoon thyme
- 2 lb chicken breast
- 6 cups instant grits, prepared

EQUIPMENT
- Dutch oven or
- Large pot and skillet
- Tray for flour coating

DIRECTIONS

1. Heat the dutch oven (or skillet) over medium heat. Combine ½ cup oil and 1 cup flour to create a roux. Cook 8-10 minutes until roux is warm caramel brown. You will start to smell it cooking. Add onion, peppers to the roux. Sauté until onions are tender. Then add garlic and cook for an additional minute. If using a skillet, transfer to a large hot pot on medium heat.

2. Add chicken broth, tomato paste, tomatoes, paprika and bay leaves. Bring to boil then reduce heat and simmer while you cook the chicken.

3. For flour dip – combine 1/4 cup flour, garlic salt, oregano, red and black pepper in a tray. Dredge (meaning coat) chicken in flour mixture.

4. Heat skillet over medium heat. Add 1 tablespoon oil to skillet. Brown the chicken, about 5 minutes. Do not overcrowd the skillet by cooking in batches. Add additional oil to the pan between batches as needed.

5. Put the browned chicken in the broth mixture. Cover and simmer for 5-10 minutes. Keep an eye on the moisture level. The mixture will be thick, but should not be dry. Add water as needed.

Putting it together:

6. Remove bay leaves. Place prepared grits in a bowl. Pour chicken creole over grits and serve.

Chicken Piccata

PREP TIME	OVEN TEMP	COOK TIME	SERVES
15min	400F	40 min	4

Traditional chicken piccata- you'll want to serve this dish every night.

INGREDIENTS
- 4 skinless/boneless chicken breasts
- Kosher salt and black pepper
- ½ cup all-purpose flour
- 6 tablespoons unsalted butter
- 4 tablespoons olive oil
- 1 lemon
- 2 cloves garlic chopped
- ½ cup white wine
- 3 tablespoons capers, drained
- ⅓ cup fresh parsley

EQUIPMENT
- Skillet

DIRECTIONS

1. Place chicken breast between two sheets of plastic and using a mallot pound until ½" thick. Cut in half crosswise. So you have 8 pieces. Salt and pepper.

2. Dredge chicken in flour and shake off excess.

3. Heat a large skillet over medium high heat. Add 2 tablespoons of butter and olive oil each. Add 3-4 piecees of chicken, browning both sides, cooking through, about 4-5 minutes per side. Remove chicken and keep warm on a plate. Add additional tablespoon of butter and oil and repeat with remaining chicken.

4. In the skillet, whisk together the juice of one lemon (about 3 tablespoons), wine, garlic and capers. Bring to boil and deglaze the pan. Reduce liquid by 1/3.

5. Return the chicken to the pan and turn heat down to a simmer for 3-5 minutes.

Putting it all together:

6. Remove chicken from pan and place on plate. Add another tablespoon of butter to sauce and whisk while butter melting to fully combine. Pour sauce over chicken. Garnish with parsley and lemon zest.

Wondering what to serve it with?

Place chicken on bed of pasta or rice before adding sauce then add a green veggie like asparagus!

Steak & Fries

PREP TIME	OVEN TEMP	COOK TIME	SERVES
20 min	425F	45 min	4

Fancy enough for company but easy enough for a weeknight! The butter sauce *makes* this recipe.

INGREDIENTS
- Vegetable oil
- Olive oil
- 3-4 medium russet potatoes
- 4 strip steaks
- 2 large shallots minced
- ⅓ cup dry white wine
- 1 teaspoon lemon juice
- ½ tablespoon white wine vinegar
- ½ cup unsalted butter, soft
- 1 tablespoon fresh tarragon
- 1 tablespoon fresh oregano
- 1 tablespoon fresh parsley
- Salt and pepper

EQUIPMENT
- Deep pan/Large Pot
- Skillet
- Cookie Sheet

DIRECTIONS

1. Peel potatoes and cut into thin strips. Rinse under water to remove starch. Place in pot and cover with cold water. Parboil potatoes for 3-5 minutes. Drain and pat dry or water will cause the grease to pop.

2. Heat 1½ to 2 inches oil in a deep pan over medium heat to 400F degrees. Gently place small batches of potatoes into hot oil. Cook for 3-5 minutes and transfer to a towel lined plate. Pre-heat oven to 425F.

3. Season both sides of steaks with salt and pepper. Heat skillet over high heat. Add about 1 tablespoon of olive oil to pan. Sear both sides- just to give it a crisp outside and seal in juices. Lower the heat to a medium and continue cooking until desired doneness 6-10 minutes (see index). Remove steaks and place on plate, cover with foil to rest 10 minutes and keep warm.

4. Infuse the shallots with additional flavor by soaking them with wine, lemon juice and vinegar. Let soak for 5 minutes. Then drain off excess liquid. Add softened butter, and herbs into bowl with shallots and whip thoroughly. Salt and pepper to taste.

Putting it together:

5. Spread fries on cookie sheet, season with salt and place in pre-heated oven for 4 minutes to crisp up, turning once. Meanwhile, slice steak into 1/4-inch slices on the bias and lay on platter – leaving about 1/3 of the platter open for fries. Spread some of the butter sauce across the middle of the slices – it should start to melt and sink into the meat. Add the fries to the open part of the platter. Serve immediately.

Chicken Lettuce Wraps

PREP TIME 20 min **MARINADE** 30min-2hr **COOK TIME** 10 min **SERVES** 4

A fresh low-carb dinner that's fun to eat. Lettuce wraps have a distinct Asian flavor and would go great with some edamame, broccoli or pea pods.

INGREDIENTS

3 chicken breasts
¼ cup hoisin sauce
¼ cup soy sauce
1½ teaspoons minced ginger
1 teaspoon sweet chili sauce
1 tablespoon rice wine vinegar
1 teaspoon garlic
½ teaspoon cilantro
2 teaspoons peanut oil
¼ teaspoon sesame oil
Lettuce leaves
Rice noodles, prepare according to package

Sauce
2 tablespoons Soy sauce
2 tablespoons Hoisin sauce
2 tablespoons Chili sauce

EQUIPMENT
Cookie sheet
Skillet

No rice wine vinegar?

Try White wine vinegar instead. You can also substitute Sriracha for Chili Sauce.

DIRECTIONS

1. Marinade: mix hoisin, soy, ginger, chili sauce, vinegar, and garlic together in a bowl. Set aside. Cut the chicken breast into ½" cubes. Wondering how? Slice the chicken in half, like you are butterflying it, but cut all the way through. Then cut each half into long strips about ½ wide. Finally chop each strip into ½ inch pieces. Try to make them the same size for better cooking.

2. Place chicken in the marinade. Place in refrigerator and marinate for 30 min – 2 hours

3. Pan Fry – Heat large skillet over medium high heat. Add oil to the pan with just a ½ teaspoon of Sesame oil – not too much, the flavor is strong. Cook the chicken in batches and place cooked chicken on a plate. OR Oven cook – Heat oven to 350F. Spread chicken on non-stick pan and spray lightly with cooking spray. Cook 7-9 minutes until cooked.

4. Sauce: use equal parts of soy, hoisin and chili sauce to create sauce. Use more soy for a milder sauce.

Putting it together:

5. Sprinkle chicken with cilantro and serve alongside lettuce leaves, noodles and sauce. Use the lettuce leaf as a "shell" and wrap the chicken, noodles and sauce in it.

Quick Pizza Dough

PREP TIME 15 min **RISE TIME** 30 min **COOK TIME** 40 min **OVEN TEMP** 475F **YIELDS** 2 12" rounds

Make your own pizza night is always a favorite in our house! This dough is quick and easy and could be made by the kids.

INGREDIENTS
- 1 cup warm water 105-110F
- 1 tablespoon sugar
- 1 tablespoon active dry yeast
- 1 tablespoon olive oil
- 2 - 2½ cups flour
- 1 teaspoon salt
- ¼ teaspoon garlic salt
- Additional olive oil

EQUIPMENT
- Stand mixer
- Pizza stone

DIRECTIONS

1. Pre Heat oven to 475F. Place pizza stone in oven to heat up.

2. In a stand mixer, Stir yeast and sugar into the warm water. Proof (let sit) 5 min, until frothy. This gives the yeast a head start on activating.

3. Mix salt and olive oil into the yeast. Slowly add 2 cups of flour. Add additional flour 1 tablespoon at a s time as needed until ball forms. Scrape down sides of bowl. Blend at medium speed for 3 min. Dough will still be a little tacky but it will not be stick all over your fingers.

4. Transfer dough to floured surface and form into a smooth ball.

5. If you have time, allow the dough to rise in a covered bowl coated with olive oil for about 30 min. This does produce a slightly airier dough.

6. Cut dough in half and massage each half into 12-inch rounds. Place on a piece of parchment paper and "dock" crust with a fork, poking holes about every inch to keep large bubbles or too much rising. Add sauce, cheese and desired toppings. Brush the crust with olive oil and sprinkle crust with a touch of garlic salt.

Putting it together:

7. Gently slide pizza on parchment paper onto hot pizza stone. Cook for 8 min or until golden brown.

Pizza Dough a little soggy?

If you like a lot of toppings, dough can get soggy. Try par-baking dough, 2-3 minutes, before adding toppings.

Quick Pizza Sauce

PREP TIME 15 min   **MAKES** 2 cups

The real difference between pizza sauce and a pasta sauce is pizza sauce is an uncooked tomato sauce and pasta sauce is cooked!

INGREDIENTS
- 3-4 large fresh tomatoes
- ¼ teaspoon oregano
- 2 teaspoons minced garlic
- ½ teaspoon salt
- ¼ teaspoon black pepper
- 12oz can tomato paste
- 2 tablespoons olive oil

EQUIPMENT
Blender (optional)

DIRECTIONS

1. Slice tomatoes in half and scoop out the seeds. Try to gently squeeze out any additional liquid. Pizza sauce should be drier than pasta sauce. Place tomatoes and all other ingredients into blender. Blend till smooth.

2. Use immediately or store refrigerated for up to one week.

Have more tomatoes?

You can use all fresh tomatoes and leave out the tomato paste if you prefer. You'll want about 12 large tomatoes

Pesto Pizza Sauce

PREP TIME 15 min   **MAKES** 1/2 cup

This sauce is slightly different than a traditional pesto to keep the crust from getting soggy. This is great topped with only fresh-sliced tomato, fresh mozzarella and basil!

INGREDIENTS
- 3 cups basil leaves
- 2-3 tablespoons olive oil
- 2 cloves garlic chopped
- ½ teaspoon salt (to taste)
- Fresh pepper

EQUIPMENT
- Blender (optional)

DIRECTIONS
1. Place basil, 2 tablespoons olive oil, garlic and salt in a blender. Blend until smooth. Add salt and pepper to taste.

2. Best when used immediately.

No Basil?

Substitute Parsley, Tarragon, Arugula even Spinach.

Lemon Chicken

PREP TIME	OVEN TEMP	COOK TIME	SERVES
15 min	400F	30 min	4-6

What's not to love about lemons? Lemon chicken is full of flavor and bursting with freshness. It doesn't take long but you will fall in love with this dish. And the leftovers make great chicken salad!

INGREDIENTS

- 1 tablespoon olive oil
- 2 tablespoons minced garlic
- ⅓ cup white wine (or chicken broth)
- Zest from 1 lemon
- 2 tablespoons lemon juice
- 1½ teaspoons dried oregano
- ½ teaspoon lemon pepper
- 1 teaspoon coriander
- ½ teaspoon thyme
- Kosher salt
- Black pepper
- 4 boneless chicken breasts
- 1 lemon, wedged
- Parsley

EQUIPMENT

- Saucepan
- 9x13 baking dish

DIRECTIONS

1. Preheat the oven to 400F.

2. Create a garlic oil by heating olive oil in a small saucepan over low heat, add garlic and sauté just until you begin to smell it – about 1 minute. You don't want the garlic to brown. Removed from heat.

3. Sauce: To the garlic oil, add the white wine, lemon zest, lemon juice, oregano, coriander, lemon pepper, thyme, and 1 teaspoon salt. Stir to mix and pour into the baking dish.

4. Brush each chicken breast lightly with olive oil and lay chicken on top of the sauce. Sprinkle with salt and pepper.

5. Bake at 400F for 30 minutes-until the chicken is 165F internally. Don't overcook, it will dry out the chicken. Remove from oven and cover the pan tightly with aluminum foil. Let the chicken rest for about 10 minutes to reabsorb juices.

Putting it all together:

6. Serve chicken directly from the pan since it will have cooled. Or you can place on a bed of rice, drizzling with sauce from the pan. Add a touch more salt and pepper to taste.

Classic Crab Cakes

PREP TIME	OVEN TEMP	COOK TIME	SERVES
30 min	optional	30 min	8-12

Crab cakes can be intim but not these! There are a couple of easy steps, then just fry them up in a pan. You can create this delicious dish in no time!

INGREDIENTS

Mayonnaise:
- ½ cup store-bought mayo
- 2 teaspoons Worcestershire
- 2 teaspoons hot sauce
- 1 tablespoon Dijon mustard
- ¾ teaspoon paprika
- ½ teaspoon thyme
- ¼ teaspoon dill

Crab cake:
- 5 cups bread crumbs
- ½ cup chopped parsley
- ¼ cup chopped green onions
- ½ chopped red bell peppers
- 1 pound crabmeat, drained
- 2 tablespoons butter
- 2 tablespoons olive oil
- Lemon, sliced

EQUIPMENT
- Skillet
- Tray for breading

DIRECTIONS

1. Whisk in a bowl the mayonnaise with the other ingredients. Set aside.

2. Mix breadcrumbs and parsley in tray for breading. Reserve 1 Cup. Combine crabmeat, onions, peppers and prepared mayo until just blended. Gently add the reserved breadcrumb mixture. You want the mixture to be moist but stick together. Do not overwork the crabmeat.

3. Form the crab mixture into patties and dredge both sides in breadcrumbs mixture. Chill in fridge for 1 hour (optional) Heat skillet over medium high heat. Melt 1 tablespoon of butter and 1 tablespoon olive oil – do not let butter brown! Add crab cakes without crowding pan. Cooking about 4-5 minutes on each side. Repeat as needed to cook all crab cakes. Crab cakes should reach an internal temp of 155F or more to kill bacteria.

Putting it together:

4. Transfer Crab cakes to platter, drizzle with lemon juice and serve with parsley sprigs and several slices of lemon. Include a remoulade sauce if desired (store bought or Remoulade recipe page 28).

Make your own using 1 egg yolk, 2 teaspoon of lemon juice and 1 additional tablespoon of mustard. Blend with other ingredients listed in food processor and drizzle in 5-6 tablespoons of oil to create a mayonnaise.

Pepper Steak

PREP TIME 10 min   **COOK TIME** 20 min   **SERVES** 6

This pepper steak stir fry is quick but delicious! Simply a thinly sliced flank steak and peppers in a garlic-ginger sauce.

INGREDIENTS
- 1 tablespoon vegetable oil
- 1 red bell pepper
- 1 green bell pepper
- 1 pound flank steak thin sliced
- 2 teaspoons minced garlic
- 1 teaspoon minced ginger
- ½ teaspoon ground ginger
- ¼ cup soy sauce
- 1½ tablespoons sugar
- 1 ounce Bourbon (optional)
- 1½ tablespoons cornstarch
- Salt and pepper to taste

Optional marinade
- ⅓ cup vegetable oil
- ¼ cup soy sauce
- 2 tablespoons lemon/lime juice
- 2 tablespoons brown sugar

Prefer fried rice?
Serve steak and peppers in a bowl alongside a bowl of fresh fried rice (recipe page 39). Fry the rice while the steak cooks.

DIRECTIONS

OPTIONAL marinade: Combine the marinade ingredients into a bowl. Slice the flank steak into thin slices and add to the bowl. Let marinade for 30 minutes. Discard marinade.

1. Slice Peppers into thin strips. Cut flank steak into thin slices and season well with salt and pepper. Heat pan over medium high heat. Add a small amount of oil to pan (½-1 teaspoon). Add the peppers and cook for 3-4 minutes or until just tender. Remove and set aside. Increase the heat on the pan and add another teaspoon of oil. Add steak to the pan and cook for 5-6 minutes, just until pink is gone.

2. Lower heat back down. Add the garlic and ginger, then cook for 30 seconds. Add bourbon (optional). Place the peppers back in the pan with the steak and toss.

3. In a small bowl, whisk together the soy sauce, sugar, 1/4 cup water and cornstarch. Pour the sauce over the steak mixture and simmer on medium heat. Cook until sauce has just thickened.

Putting it all together:
5. Place white in a large bowl and spoon steak and peppers onto rice.

One Pan Chicken

PREP TIME	OVEN TEMP	COOK TIME	SERVES
15 min	425F	25 min	6

What can be better than only one pan to clean?

INGREDIENTS
- ¼ cup balsamic vinegar
- 1 cup olive oil
- 1 tablespoon fresh basil
- 1 tablespoon oregano
- 1 teaspoon kosher salt
- ½ teaspoon black pepper
- 5 cloves garlic, minced
- 8 skin-on chicken thighs
- ½ red onion
- 1 pound green beans
- 2 cups mixed cherry tomatoes
- 1 tablespoon fresh parsley

EQUIPMENT
Large cookie sheet

DIRECTIONS
1. Preheat the oven to 425F.

2. Whisk together olive oil, basil, salt, pepper, and garlic. Place chicken and about half of the olive oil mixtures in bowl to marinate.

3. Toss the green beans, onion and cherry tomatoes in a bowl with the remaining marinade.

4. Remove chicken from the bag and place spaced apart on a large cookie sheet – skin side up if skin-on. Arrange green bean mixture around the chicken, being careful not to add the marinade to the cookie sheet.

5. Roast for 25-30 minutes, depending on size of chicken pieces. Check for browned chicken and temperature doneness.

Putting it all together:

6. You can serve directly from your pan or move to a platter. Sprinkle with salt and pepper if needed, add some fresh parsley.

Make this dish your own?

This dish is super flexible! Add carrots, root veggies or whatever you have available. Just watch the cook time or make thin slice so they cook as fast as the chicken.

Salmon with Herb Butter

PREP TIME	REST TIME	COOK TIME	SERVES
5 min	20 min optional	15 min	4

This recipe is light and flavorful. No reason to fear fish!
You can do this.

INGREDIENTS
4 salmon fillets
1 cup milk (optional)
3 tablespoons butter, divided
2 teaspoons minced garlic
2 teaspoons lemon juice
1 teaspoon fresh parsley
1 teaspoon dill
Salt and pepper

EQUIPMENT
Skillet

DIRECTIONS

OPTIONAL: Soak 20 minutes in milk if you need to remove a fishy smell. Rinse and pat dry.

1. Sprinkle salmon filets with salt and pepper.

2. Add 1 tablespoon butter to hot non-stick pan. Then add salmon, skin side down. Cook for 5-7 minutes depending on thickness. Gently flip and sear the top side for about 2 minutes and then flip back to the skin side.

3. Add into the skillet 2 tablespoon butter, minced garlic, lemon juice, fresh parsley and dill. Let cook then spoon over salmon fillets.

Putting it all together:
4. Plate salmon on individual plates and spoon sauce over salmon. Works well with grilled or steamed green vegetables. Try the lemon roasted asparagus (recipe page 35)

Have frozen salmon?

That's OK! Cover the skillet and let the fish steam for 10 minutes or so. Then uncover and cook off excess moisture.

Lemon Thyme Cream Sauce

PREP TIME	COOK TIME	SERVES
10 min	10 min	6

A delicious sauce to dress up an average dinner -- use on chicken or fish.

INGREDIENTS
- 2 tablespoons butter
- 1 clove garlic minced
- 1 tablespoon green onion
- 1 cup chicken broth
- 1 teaspoon flour
- ½ cup half and half
- Salt and pepper to taste
- 1 tablespoon chopped thyme
- 1 teaspoon parsley
- 1 lemon zest and juice

EQUIPMENT
Saucepan

DIRECTIONS

1. Heat a pan over medium heat. Melt butter then add garlic and green onion and cook until you smell the garlic – don't let it brown. Add the chicken broth, simmering for 2-3 minutes.

2. Whisk the flour into the half and half. Then whisk into pan. Cook for one minute.

3. Add in thyme and lemon juice. Bring to a gentle boil, and stirring occasionally until slightly thickened.

Putting it together:

4. Add the lemon zest and then season to taste with salt and pepper. Drizzle cream sauce over chicken or fish.

No time?

Slice up a store-bought rotisserie chicken or use frozen tilapia, cooking in 425F oven until flaky, 8-10 minutes.

Dress it up with this cream sauce. Maybe add a little garnish of thyme or parsley.

Barbecued Shrimp

PREP TIME 15 min   **COOK TIME** 15 min   **SERVES** 6

This staple of New Orleans is a spicy and delicious black pepper spiced butter sauce. The spices give it a slight orange tint, like BBQ. You'll never think of barbecue the same way!

INGREDIENTS
- 1 pound large shrimp in shells
- 1 tablespoon olive oil
- 1 tablespoon black pepper
- 1 teaspoon cayenne pepper
- 2 teaspoons creole seasoning
- 1 teaspoon oregano
- 1 stick unsalted butter
- 1½ teaspoons minced garlic
- 2 tablespoons Worcestershire sauce
- ½ juice from lemon
- 2 tablespoons white wine

EQUIPMENT
Large Skillet

DIRECTIONS

1. Rinse shrimp off in cold water. Remove heads if still attached but do not peel. Cut lemon in half.

2. In a large skillet, on high heat oil, heat oil then add garlic. Combine Worcestershire sauce, peppers and creole seasoning and add to skillet for 1 minute. Then add wine, lemon juice and peel into skillet and all shrimp. Cook, turning for about 2 minutes. You will see the shrimp start to turn pink.

3. Begin adding the butter to the pan a tablespoon at a time. "Stir" the sauce by shaking the pan back and forth. Continue cooking for 2-3 more minutes. The sauce will begin to thicken and darken and the shrimp will be pink and opaque.

4. Total cooking time should be 5-6 minutes depending on size of shrimp. You do not want to overcook.

Putting it all together:

5. Serve the shrimp immediately with good crusty French bread, to sop up the delicious sauce or over angel hair pasta. Add a couple of slices of lemon as garnish. Don't forget an extra bowl for the discarded shells and lots of extra napkins.

I can't make this better!

It is truly delicious stand-alone! A great choice for dessert would be traditional banana's foster!

Makka's Tilapia with Tomato-Cream Sauce

PREP TIME	COOK TIME	SERVES
15 min	15 min	4

Believe it or not this dish is really kid friendly. The flavors are so mild and the tilapia is flaky and soft. A great option to get kids eating more fish.

INGREDIENTS
- 4 Tilapia filets
- Water
- ½ cup white wine
- 15 grape tomatoes, halved (or 3 large tomatoes diced)
- ½ cup heavy cream
- 1 teaspoon cornstarch
- 1 teaspoon thyme
- Salt and pepper

EQUIPMENT
- Skillet with lid

DIRECTIONS

1. Season filets with salt and pepper. Heat skillet over low heat. Add wine and enough water to fill about ½ inch in skillet. Heat water to 140-145F. Do not simmer or boil. Add tomatoes to skillet.

2. Place filets in skillet and cover. Cook slowly on low heat for about 5-7 minutes, depending on thickness of fish.

3. Gently remove from pan and place on plate, covering to keep warm.

4. Increase heat on skillet. Reduce water by half. Combine cream and cornstarch, mix thoroughly. Then add to cream mixture and thyme to pan. Bring just to boil.

Putting it all together:

5. Place fish on individual plates and spoon sauce with tomatoes over each filet. Garnish with parsley or lemon slices.

Fish Frozen?

No Problem! Fish cooks well straight from the freezer. Just rinse under cool water to get rid of water crystals.

Roast Beef Dip Sandwiches

PREP TIME	ROAST TIME	COOK TIME	SERVES
15 min	6-8 hours	15 min	6

This is a hearty cool weather option. Serve with a side of soup or a salad.

INGREDIENTS
- 2 cups beef broth
- 1 cup red wine (optional)
- 2 tablespoons Worcestershire Sauce
- 1 tablespoon onion, small dice
- 1 teaspoon minced garlic
- 1½ teaspoons salt
- 1 teaspoon black pepper
- 1½ teaspoon dried oregano
- 1 teaspoon ground thyme
- 1 bay leaf
- 3-4 lbs. beef chuck roast
- Butter
- 16 slices Provolone/Swiss/Jack
- 16 slices of Sourdough/French bread (Sara Lee Artisan's great)

EQUIPMENT
- Slow cooker crockpot
- Skillet

DIRECTIONS

1. Trim excess fat off roast. Salt and pepper both sides of roast.

2. Optional This step adds more depth of flavor to your roast, but is not required for a delicious sandwich. Dredge the roast in flour and place in a skillet on medium-high heat. Brown exterior of roast -about 2 minutes on each side.

3. Place roast in crockpot. Mix broth, wine and spices into the pot. If you choose not to use red wine, add one additional cup of broth or water.

4. Slow cook on low heat for 6-8 hours. Stick a fork into the meat and see if you can pull out a small piece - the meat should easily come apart.

5. Remove meat from crockpot but reserve juices. Skim fat off the top of juices. Shred the meat and then return to pot and sauce.

Putting it all together:

6. Heat skillet over medium heat. Butter one side of the bread slices. Lay a piece of cheese on the unbuttered side of the bread. Using a slotted spoon, drain the meat and place a heaping spoonful onto the cheese. Top with another slice of cheese and then bread, butter-side out. Toast both sides of the sandwich in skillet until cheese melted - like you would a grilled cheese. Pour remaining juices into a bowl for au jus. Serve immediately.

BBQ Beef Brisket

PREP TIME	MARINATE	COOK TIME	SERVES
5 min	5 hours	6 hours	8

Traditional Texas brisket – the original barbecue! This cut of meat has to slow cook in order to be tender and delicious. So plan ahead!

INGREDIENTS

- 3½-4 lb. beef brisket
- ½ cup brown sugar
- 1 tablespoon paprika
- 2 tablespoons smoked paprika
- 4 teaspoons black pepper
- 3 tablespoons kosher salt
- 1 tablespoon garlic powder
- 1 tablespoon onion powder
- 1 teaspoon mustard powder
- 2 teaspoons cumin
- 1 teaspoon oregano
- 1 teaspoon cayenne (or more)
- Barbecue sauce

EQUIPMENT

Cookie sheet

DIRECTIONS

1. Trim large pieces of fat or white strands from brisket. You can leave about ½ inch of fat. It will cook down.

2. Mix all spices in a bowl. Rub brisket liberally with spices on all sides. Refrigerate for 4 hours-overnight.

3. Remove brisket from refrigerator and set on counter for about 1 hour to get meat to room temperature.

4. Wrap meat tightly in a couple layers of foil to keep juices in. Lay on a cookie sheet to save your oven from the drips.

5. Cook 300F 1.25 hour/pound (until 185 internal)Then lower to 250, baste with BBQ sauce and cook another hour (try to get to 200 and keep it there). When sliced, you will notice the meat is no longer pink. For a brisket, that's good! Let rest 30 minutes.

Putting it together:
7. Slice across the grain. Place sliced brisket by a plate or on rolls with additional barbecue sauce. Serve with cole slaw or salad.

Using a different cut of meat?

Beef chuck roast works well too and will shred beautifully. May need extra cooking.

Nashville-Style Hot Chicken

PREP TIME 20 min | **COOK TIME** 25 min | **SERVES** 6

Have you tried Hot Chicken yet? Best thing to happen to fried chicken in years!

INGREDIENTS

Dry Brine:
- 2 tablespoons kosher salt
- 1 teaspoons black pepper
- 3-4 large chicken breasts

Dredge:
- 1 egg
- 1 cup buttermilk
- 1 tablespoon hot sauce
- 2 cups all-purpose flour
- ¾ cup cornstarch
- 1 tablespoon salt
- 1 tablespoon black pepper
- 3-4 cups vegetable shortening

Spicy Sauce:
- ½ cup grease from pan (or shortening, melted)
- 1 tablespoon cayenne
- 1 tablespoon paprika
- 1 tablespoon brown sugar
- 1 teaspoon salt
- ½ teaspoon black pepper
- 1 teaspoon garlic powder

EQUIPMENT
- Shallow trays/dish
- Large pot for deep frying

DIRECTIONS

Dry Brine:

1. Cut chicken breasts in half width wise and length wise. These will cook more evenly and will fit perfectly on a biscuit or on white bread. Toss chicken in 2 tablespoons salt, 1 teaspoon black pepper to coat. Set in refrigerator to dry brine for 3 hours till overnight.

Remove from refrigerator.

Cooking Chicken:

2. Heat shortening in a deep pot to 350F. There should be 1-2 inches of oil. Set up a wire rack on a cookie sheet for the cooked chicken.

3. In a shallow tray combine eggs, buttermilk and hot sauce. In a second tray combine flour, cornstarch, salt and pepper.

4. Dredge each piece of chicken in the flour mixture then dip in the buttermilk mixture. Repeat this 1-2 more times to coat chicken. Lay on foil to rest for 10 minutes.

5. Once shortening is 350F, place chicken gently into hot oil. Cook for 3-4 minutes and gently turn over. It should be browned on both sides. Place lid on skillet for

Nashville-Style Hot Chicken

PREP TIME	COOK TIME	SERVES
15 min	15 min	6

3 minutes to steam chicken. Remove lid and then remove chicken from skillet.

Lay chicken on wire rack to drain. Repeat with remaining pieces of chicken. Sauce:
6. Melt the butter and allow to cool. Whisk in the dry ingredients. Then add 1/4 grease to thin.   Brush on top of chicken pieces.

Putting it together:
7. Serve the chicken on a biscuit or bun. Lay chicken on the bread, be sure you have plenty of sauce brushed on it and add a pickle if desired.

Cooking for kids?

Leave some chicken breasts "dry" without the spicy sauce. The meat is still juicy, tender and full of flavor. If you prefer reduce the heat by adding some honey to the biscuit and chicken.

Spaghetti Sauce

PREP TIME	COOK TIME	SERVES
15 min	1 hour	6

This spaghetti sauce will stand up to any noodle. It's also great to make ahead and freeze for those nights you just don't feel like cooking.

INGREDIENTS
- 10-12 large fresh tomatoes (2-14 oz cans crushed tomato)
- 1 teaspoon olive oil
- 1 medium onion
- 2 teaspoons mince garlic
- 2 bay leaves
- 1 cup water or beef stock
- ¼ cup red wine (optional)
- ¼ cup brown sugar
- ¼ teaspoon cinnamon
- 2 tablespoon fresh basil
- 1 tablespoon fresh oregano
- 1 tablespoon fresh parsley
- 2 teaspoons salt
- ½ teaspoon pepper
- pinch of red pepper
- 1 tablespoon fresh basil
- Grated Parmesan cheese

EQUIPMENT
- Large Pot with lid
- Food Processor

DIRECTIONS

1. Chop onion, pepper and garlic to a very small dice. Roughly chop herbs

2. Peel (optional)* core and seed the tomatoes. Then place in food processor and chop not quite to purée.

3. In a large pot, heat olive oil over medium heat. Add onions until soft and translucent. Add garlic. Cook for 1 minute.

4. Add tomatoes, bay leaves, water, wine, brown sugar, cinnamon and herbs and spices. Bring to a simmer. Cover and cook for 15-20 minutes. Taste sauce for salt and spice levels.

5. If you are adding meatballs, add them to sauce and simmer uncover for 5-8 minutes before serving.

Putting it together:

6. Serve tomato sauce over pasta of your choice. Sprinkle with fresh chopped basil and grated Parmesan cheese.

How do you peel a tomato?

Cut a large "X" on the bottom of each tomato. Place in ot of boiling water for about 3 minutes. You are not trying to cook the tomato. You'll see skin start to peel and wrinkle. Drain and rinse with cold water. Then peel the skin off.

Meatballs for Spaghetti

PREP TIME	OVEN TEMP	COOK TIME	SERVES
10 min	400F	12 min	4

Classic meatballs-- perfect for dressing up spaghetti night.

INGREDIENTS
- 1 lb. ground beef
- 2 teaspoons Worcestershire sauce
- ⅓ cup seasoned bread crumbs
- ¼ cup finely chopped parsley
- 1 egg, beaten
- 2 teaspoons minced garlic
- ½ teaspoon red pepper
- 1 teaspoon kosher salt
- ¼ teaspoon black pepper
- ¼ cup grated Parmesan (optional)

EQUIPMENT
Cookie sheet

DIRECTIONS

1. Combine all spices in a bowl. Beat in egg and Worcestershire sauce. Gently work into the ground beef.

2. Roll into 1-inch balls.

3. Place on cookie sheet and cook in a 400F oven for 10-12 min or until cooked.

Putting it all together:

4. Serve over spaghetti with a traditional tomato sauce. Add a sprig of basil or parsley for garnish. Don't forget the grated Parmesan and crusty bread.

Want an appetizer

Try serving these in a warm sweet sauce. Warm 3/4 cup grape jelly with 1 1/2 cup ketchup and add these meatballs without the cheese!

Dippin' Chicken

PREP TIME	OVEN TEMP	COOK TIME	SERVES
15 min	375F	10 min	4

This is a favorite of my kids. Finger food always is! It doesn't take long and they can pick their favorite sauces to eat.

INGREDIENTS
- 4 chicken breasts
- ½ cup flour
- 1 teaspoon garlic powder
- Vegetable spray like Pam®
- Salt and pepper
- Toothpicks
- Favorite sauces (BBQ, Teriyaki)

EQUIPMENT
- Cookie Sheet

DIRECTIONS

1. Line cookie sheet with foil and spray foil with vegetable spray.

2. Slice chicken into 1-inch cubes. Slice chicken in half width-wise, like you are butterflying the chicken breast. Then slice into 1-inch strips. Finally slice into 1-inch cubes. It's important to make the pieces as uniform as possible.

3. Lightly season the pieces with salt and pepper.

4. Combine the flour and garlic powder in a bowl. Dredge the chicken pieces in the flour mixture. Shake off excess. Then spread chicken on cookie sheet. Spray chicken liberally with vegetable spray.

5. Bake chicken at 375F for about 10 min. Check chicken for doneness after 8 minutes. Do not overcook or the chicken will be dry.

Putting it together:

6. Put the chicken on a platter. Place tooth picks in several of the pieces and provide additional toothpicks. Serve with an assortment of your favorite sauces, like BBQ, Teriyaki and honey mustard.

Kid friendly dinner night?

Try cooking with the roasted broccoli or roasted potatoes; both are quick and easy.

Southern Pork BBQ

PREP TIME 10 min   **COOK TIME** 6-8 hours   **SERVES** 8

There are so many versions of BBQ depending on what part of the country you're from. But don't let that stop you from trying this version, you may find you like it too!

INGREDIENTS
- 3 lb. pork butt (shoulder)
- ½ cup apple cider vinegar
- 2 bay leaves
- ¼ cup brown sugar
- 1 tablespoon coriander
- 1 tablespoon paprika
- 1 tablespoon Worcestershire
- 2 teaspoons garlic powder
- 2 teaspoons kosher salt
- 1 teaspoon black pepper
- 1 teaspoon cayenne pepper
- 1 teaspoon ground mustard
- 2 onions, cut into halves

EQUIPMENT
Crock Pot

DIRECTIONS

1. Mix brown sugar, coriander, paprika, mustard, garlic, salt, peppers together.

2. Rub on all sides of pork to coat.

3. Place Onions in bottom of crock pot. Set pork on top of onions. Add vinegar, Worcestershire, bay leaves and enough water to cover the meat.

4. Cook in crock pot on low for 8-12 hours (or on high for 5-6 hours). Meat should easily tear apart.

5. Remove from pot and shred pork using two forks.

Putting it together:
6. Place heaping spoonfuls of meat on to hamburger buns. Add your favorite BBQ sauce and a pickle slice.

What to serve it with?

Good Southern BBQ is always served with a cole slaw.

Buffalo Wings

PREP TIME	OVEN TEMP	COOK TIME	SERVES
15 min	375F	40 min	4

Don't let the "buffalo" scare you away. They do rock a little spice, but they are still finger lickin' good!

INGREDIENTS
1 package of chicken wings (about 12)
Peanut oil
1 stick butter
1 teaspoon minced garlic
1 bottle hot sauce
½ teaspoon lemon juice
1 teaspoon Worcestershire

EQUIPMENT
Large saucepan for frying
Cookie Sheet- foil lined
Small saucepan for sauce

DIRECTIONS

1. Rinse wings off and pat dry. Separate each wing into two parts at the joint to make a drumette and a flat piece.

2. Heat 3" of peanut oil in large saucepan to 350F. Cook the wing pieces in batches, frying until they are fully cooked (165F internal). Set on paper towel lined plate to drain.

3. Meanwhile, in a small saucepan, melt the butter over low heat. Add the hot sauce, garlic, lemon and Worcestershire sauce and stir until it begins to boil. Remove from heat.

4. Toss cooked wings in sauce and lay on cookie sheet.

5. Bake chicken in 375F oven for 10-15 minutes.

Putting it together:
6. Place wings in a basket or platter, garnish with celery and blue cheese and ranch dressings.

Teriyaki Wings

PREP TIME	OVEN TEMP	COOK TIME	SERVES
15 min	375F	40 min	4

This is a fun variation we first tasted a little hole in the wall restaurant in Boston. We had to come home and try them right away.

INGREDIENTS
1 package of chicken wings (about 12)
Peanut oil
1 cup soy sauce
2 tablespoon rice vinegar
½ cup honey
½ cup water
1 teaspoon sesame oil
1 tablespoon mince ginger
1 tablespoon minced garlic
2 teaspoons cornstarch
1 tablespoon green onions

EQUIPMENT
Large saucepan for frying
Cookie Sheet- foil lined
Small saucepan for sauce

DIRECTIONS

1. Rinse wings off and pat dry. Separate each wing into two parts at the joint to make a drumette and a flat piece.

2. Heat 3" of peanut oil in large saucepan to 350F. Cook the wing pieces in batches, frying until they are fully cooked (165F internal). Set on paper towel lined plate to drain.

3. Whisk together the soy sauce and cornstarch. In a small saucepan, mix vinegar, honey, water, sesame oil, ginger, garlic and garlic. Stir until it begins to boil. Remove from heat and whisk in the soy sauce mixture.

4. Toss cooked wings in sauce and lay on cookie sheet.

5. Bake chicken in 375F oven for 10-15 minutes.

Putting it together:
6. Place wings in a basket or platter, garnish with green onions and serve with remaining sauce.

Baked Chicken with Parmesan Crust

PREP TIME	OVEN TEMP	REST TIME	COOK TIME	SERVES
15 min	450F	30 min	15 min	4

Since you can marinate this overnight, it's a great dish to bake up on short notice! just coat it inthe cheese mixture and bake. Whew! Dinner done fast.

INGREDIENTS

- 2 tablespoons Italian Dressing
- ½ teaspoon thyme leaves
- ½ teaspoon oregano
- ¼ teaspoon pepper
- 4 boneless, skinless chicken breast halves (about 8 ounces each)
- ¾ cup parmesan cheese
- ¾ cup bread crumbs

EQUIPMENT

- Cookie Sheet- foil lined
- Shallow tray

DIRECTIONS

1. Preheat the oven to 450F.

2. Mix the dressing, thyme, oregano and pepper in a bowl. Toss chicken breast in mixture to coat completely. If time allows, wrap in plastic wrap and let marinate 30 minutes up to overnight.

3. In your tray, combine parmesan and bread crumbs. Dredge chicken breast in parmesan mixture. Press down on coating to ensure it is thick and sticks. Lay on lightly greased cookie sheet.

4. Bake chicken in 450F oven for 15 minutes or until done. Then give it 5 minutes under the broiler to crisp up the crust if needed. Be sure and give the chicken a few minutes to rest to reabsorb the juices.

Putting it together:

5. Serve chicken with a side of pasta and light tomato sauce, green salad and crusty bread.

Chicken dry?

Consider using dark meat to give it more moisture! Or try pan frying instead of baking.

Ramen Crusted Chicken

PREP TIME	COOK TIME	SERVES
15 min	15 min	4

This combines the best of those college meals with healthy chicken. Crunchy and yummy!

INGREDIENTS
- 1 tablespoon olive oil
- 1 tablespoon butter
- 4 chicken breasts
- 2 ramen noodle packages
- 1 teaspoon ground ginger
- ½ teaspoon black pepper
- 1 egg, beaten
- ¼ cup soy sauce
- 2 green onions, sliced

EQUIPMENT
- Skillet
- 2 shallow trays

DIRECTIONS

1. Remove seasoning packet from noodles. Place noodles in a large plastic bag and crush noodles into very small pieces. If you prefer, you can use a food processor.

2. In one tray combine egg and soy sauce. In second tray combine Ramen noodles, seasoning packet, ginger and pepper.

3. Cut chicken in half and pound out each half until about ¼ inch thick.

4. Toss chicken in egg mixture to coat and then dredge through noodle mixture. Press down on coating to ensure it is thick and sticks.

5 Heat skillet over medium high heat. Add oil and butter. Place chicken in the pan, cooking in two batches.

Putting it together:

6. Sprinkle chicken with sliced green onion and serve with fresh vegetables like the sautéed green beans (recipe page 32).

No Ramen?

Crush up Ritz-type cracker instead of ramen and proceed as directed above.

Sesame Chicken & Noodles

PREP TIME 30 min **REST TIME** 30 min **COOK TIME** 20 min **SERVES** 6

This recipe has quiet a few ingredients but the flavor is worth it.

INGREDIENTS

2 pounds chicken breasts
Marinade
¼ cup soy sauce
1 teaspoon sesame oil
1 teaspoon salt
¼ cup water
Batter:
1 egg barely beaten
1 cup ice cold water
1 cup flour
2 tablespoons cornstarch
Chicken:
1 tablespoon olive oil
½ teaspoon sesame oil
Sauce
1 teaspoon olive oil
2 teaspoons mince garlic
2 teaspoons minced ginger
3 tablespoons sugar
3/4 teaspoon chili garlic sauce
3 green onions sliced
1 teaspoon corn starch
½ cup soy sauce
1 tablespoon rice vinegar
Angel hair pasta
1 teaspoon olive oil
¼ teaspoon sesame oil
1 teaspoon parsley
1 tablespoon sesame seeds

DIRECTIONS

1. Toast sesame seeds in dry pan medium-low heat stirring until brown, about 3 minutes. Remove from heat and set aside.

2. Cut chicken into 1" cubes. Sprinkle with salt. In a bowl, mix together the marinade ingredients. Add chicken and refrigerate for 30 minutes.

3. Prepare angel hair pasta according to package and drain. Set aside.

4. Set out chicken and prepare the batter. Lightly beat the egg, just until yellow and white mix. Add water and gently stirring. Then add flour and cornstarch. Mix slowly. It will still be lumpy. Do not try to beat out the lumps.

5. Heat skillet over medium high heat. Add oils. Dredge chicken through batter and cook in skillet until browned and done. Keep warm.

6. In same skillet, heat 1 teaspoon olive oil. Then sauté garlic and ginger about 1 minute. Whisk in remaining sauce ingredients. Heat until thickened.

7. Heat a second skillet over high heat. Add 1 teaspoon olive oil and ¼ teaspoon sesame oil. Brown noodles in skillet, about 3 minutes. Toss with parsley.

Putting it together:
8. Place fried noodles in a bowl. Layer chicken on top and drizzle with soy-ginger sauce. Top with toasted sesame seeds and serve with garnish of parsley.

Easter Ham

PREP TIME	OVEN TEMP	COOK TIME	SERVES
10 min	350F	12 min/lb	varies

Traditional Easter ham with a honey-baked flavor.

INGREDIENTS
- Bone-in spiral cut ham
- 1 cup brown sugar
- ½ cup honey
- 2 tablespoons Dijon mustard
- ¼ cup orange juice or pineapple juice
- 1 teaspoon ground ginger

EQUIPMENT
- Cookie sheet
- Small saucepan

DIRECTIONS

1. Pre-Heat oven to 350F. Line cookie sheet with foil. Wrap ham in foil and lay on cookie sheet. Place in hot oven for 12 minutes/pound.

2. In a saucepan, place all ingredients and stir until just boiling.

3. 20 minutes before ham is done cooking, pull it out and baste ham with brown sugar mixture. Be sure to baste between slices.

4. Leave uncovered and cook for remaining 20 minutes. This will create that tasty crust. Be sure internal temperature reaches 130F.

Putting it together:

5. This ham is the centerpiece of any meal. Place on a large, beautiful platter. Spread out the first few slices and cut through if necessary. Serve with slice of orange or pineapple and parsley.

How big of ham?

Plan on 3/4 lb per person if it is bone-in. If there is no bone, plan on about 1/2 lb per person. But if you like leftovers, get a bigger one!

Chicken Gumbo

PREP TIME 20 min **COOK TIME** 90 min **SERVES** 8

Gumbo is a traditional dish of southern Louisiana. The variations are as endless as the alligators in the bayou. Give this kid-friendly version a try.

INGREDIENTS
- 4 chicken breasts
- 1 pack Smoked Sausage
- ½ cup plus 1 tablespoon vegetable oil
- 2 tablespoons butter
- 1 cup all-purpose flour
- 2 cups sliced okra
- ½ large onion, chopped
- 1 green bell pepper, chopped
- 4 celery ribs, sliced
- 2 quarts hot chicken broth
- 3 garlic cloves, minced
- 2 bay leaves
- 4 teaspoons Worcestershire
- 2 teaspoons Creole seasoning
- ½ teaspoon dried thyme
- 1 teaspoon parsley
- ½-1 teaspoon hot sauce
- 4 green onions, sliced
- Filé (optional)
- Hot cooked rice

EQUIPMENT
- Skillet
- Large stock pot

DIRECTIONS

1. Slice sausage in half lengthwise then slice into ½ inch slices.

2. Heat skillet over medium high heat. Add 1 tablespoon vegetable oil. Sear chicken breast on all sides. Remove from pan and lay on plate. Add sausage to skillet and brown. Remove from pan and place on paper towel-lined plate.

3. Add ½ cup oil and butter to pan, scrapping bottom of pan to loosen bits. Slowly stir in flour. Continue cooking over medium low heat, stirring until this roux turns "coffee with light cream" color. Once the roux starts to brown, it browns quickly. Do not let it burn. Remove from heat.

4. While roux is browning, In the large pot, add 1 tablespoon of oil and sauté okra, peppers, celery and onions until softened, 4-5 minutes. The okra will start to get "sticky". Add garlic for 30 seconds then add roux to okra mixture.

5. Slowly mix in hot broth, Worcestershire, creole, thyme, parsley and bay leaves. Add chicken and sausage and bring to a boil. Let simmer for 1 hour. Remove chicken. Shred chicken and return to pot with hot sauce and green onions. Add filé if desired. Cook another 30 min.

6. Place cooked rice in a bowl. Ladle large spoonfuls of gumbo with broth over rice. Sprinkle with parsley. And serve with crusty French bread (recipe page 48).

Herb Crusted Steak

PREP TIME 15 min | **COOK TIME** 15 min | **SERVES** 4

This simple steak is ready in under 30 minutes. The secret here is a mixture of spices called Herbes de Provence. It's a delightful combination of floral and savory flavors.

INGREDIENTS

- 1½ lbs steak (½ inch thick) (sirloin, ribeye, short rib)
- 2 tablespoons olive oil
- 1 teaspoon ground mustard
- 2 teaspoons Kosher salt
- ½ teaspoon black pepper
- 2 teaspoons herbes de provence
- 5 tablespoons unsalted butter, divided
- 1 tablespoon chopped chives
- ½ cup white wine
- 12 grape tomatoes, halved

EQUIPMENT

Skillet

DIRECTIONS

1. Mix together oil, mustard, herbes de Provence salt and pepper. Press mixture into steak on both sides. Let rest while pan heats up.

2. Heat skillet over medium high heat. Melt 1 tablespoon butter and add steak. Cook 5-7 minutes on each side to get a medium-rare to medium steak. Remove from heat and let rest before slicing.

3. With paper towel remove the darkened butter without scraping the bits off the bottom of the skillet. Melt 2 tablespoons butter then add chives and tomatoes. Whisk in white wine and reduce. Set aside.

Putting it together:

4. Slice steak on the bias. Spread steak onto platter and spoon sauce over steak.

Like Potatoes?

Cook some new potatoes in the microwave, then melt butter into the skillet you cooked the steak in. Toss in the potatoes to crisp then sprinkle additional herbs de Provence, salt and pepper. Serve with steak.

Honey Mustard Chicken

PREP TIME	OVEN TEMP	COOK TIME	SERVES
10 min	425F	25 min	4

Who doesn't like honey mustard? This dressed up chicken dish will be a favorite with the kids and with guests.

INGREDIENTS
- 1-1½ lb chicken thighs (more if bone-in)
- Salt and pepper
- 3 tablespoon olive oil
- 3 tablespoons butter, melted
- 3 tablespoons dijon mustard
- 1 tablespoon shallot, minced
- 1 tablespoon honey
- 4 teaspoons garlic, minced
- 2 teaspoons thyme, minced

EQUIPMENT
Casserole Dish

DIRECTIONS

1. Preheat the oven to 425 F. Spray bottom of casserole dish with cooking spray.

2. Season chicken thighs with salt and pepper.

3. Whisk remaining ingredients together. Pour 1/3 of sauce in bottom of dish.

4. Place thighs in remaining sauce and coat well. If you have time, let the chicken marinate for 1 hour.

5. Lay chicken in dish and cover with remaining sauce.

6. Bake at 425 for about 35 minutes or until done. If you are using chicken breast, cover the dish for the first 25 minutes and then cook uncovered. This will help the chicken not dry out.

Putting it together:
7. Let chicken rest a few minutes to absorb liquid. Place on platter and drizzle with sauce. Sprinkle with pepper.

Running behind?

Grab some honey mustard dressing, add ginger and thyme and cook as directed.

Curried Chicken

PREP TIME	COOK TIME	SERVES
5 min	25 min	6

The thigh meat in this dish complements the rich warm favors and keeps it super moist!

INGREDIENTS
6 chicken thighs
½ teaspoon curry powder
¼ teaspoon kosher salt
¼ teaspoon black pepper
¼ teaspoon cinnamon
1 tablespoons vegetable oil, plus 1 teaspoon
1 tablespoon butter
2 limes
½ onion, chopped
2 teaspoons curry powder
½ teaspoon cayenne
1 teaspoon cinnamon
1 teaspoon cumin
½ cup chicken stock
½ cup heavy cream
½ teaspoon cornstarch

EQUIPMENT
Skillet

Is it too spicy?
Heat in this dish comes from the cayenne pepper, but also from the curry powder and cumin.

DIRECTIONS

1. Combine curry powder, salt, pepper and cinnamon. Sprinkle over chicken thighs.

2. Heat the oil and butter in a skillet over medium heat. Add the chicken thighs - skin side down if they have skin and cook – turning once - about 5-7 minutes on each side. Set chicken on plate and keep warm.

3. Slice limes in half and sear the cut sides in the pan. Set on plate with chicken.

4. Add 1 teaspoon oil to pan if needed. Add onions and cook until tender. Add remaining spices and cook 1 minute. Pour in chicken stock. Whisk cornstarch with cream then whisk into pan.

5. Bring to a boil and reduce heat. The sauce will thicken. It should be thin enough to drizzle and thick enough to stay on when drizzled. Add additional cream if needing to thin.

Putting it together:

6. Place cooked rice on a platter or bowl. Arrange chicken on rice and lay seared limes around the edges. Drizzle sauce over chicken and sprinkle with parsley. Serve with additional sauce on the side.

> I want them to bite into a cookie, and think of me, and smile.
>
> **JAEL MCHENRY**

Desserts

Boston Creme Pie Cupcakes

PREP TIME	OVEN TEMP	COOK TIME	MAKES
10 min	375F	20 min	15

This cupcake is a grown-up spin on your average cupcake! Starts with a box mix and whips together in less than an hour.

INGREDIENTS

Cupcakes
1 box butter cake mix

Vanilla Custard
French Vanilla Instant Pudding Mix (3oz)
1 cup half and half
1 cup heavy whipping cream
2 teaspoons vanilla
¼ cup powder sugar

Ganache
8 ounces semi-sweet chocolate
1 cup heavy whipping cream
½ cup light corn syrup
1 teaspoon vanilla extract

EQUIPMENT
Muffin pan
Hand Mixer
Sauce Pan

DIRECTIONS

Cupcakes:
1. Make cupcakes according to box instructions.

Custard:
2. Mix Pudding mix and half and half. In a separate bowl, whip whipping cream, vanilla and powdered sugar until soft peaks form. Fold pudding mix into whipped cream mixture.

Ganache:
3. Heat cream in a small pot until simmering – do not boil. Pour cream over chocolate chips. Cover and let sit for 5 minutes to soften chips. Add corn syrup and vanilla and stir until melted.

Putting it all together:
4. Fill a pastry bag fitted with a 1/4-inch plain tip with the custard. Poke the tip into the top of the cupcake. Squeeze the custard into the cupcake until you see the cupcake start to expand a little. Repeat with all cupcakes. Then pour the ganache onto the center of each cupcake, using enough so the top is coated and starts to drip down the sides.

No heavy whipping cream?

Substitute 8 ounces of Cool Whip for the heavy whipping cream. Gently blend in the vanilla and powdered sugar while you blend in the pudding.

Caramel Brownies

PREP TIME	OVEN TEMP	COOK TIME	MAKES
10 min	375F	20 min	15

This is always a winner for a quick, decadent dessert. If you like caramel, you will love this!

INGREDIENTS
- German Chocolate Cake Mix
- 2/3 cup evaporated milk
- ⅓ cup butter, softened
- 1 bag caramels
- 1 cup chocolate chips

EQUIPMENT
- 9x13 pan
- sauce pan

DIRECTIONS

1. Pre-Heat oven to 375F

2. Mix by hand cake mix, ⅓ cup evaporated milk and ⅓ cup butter. It will be dry and chunky. Press ½ of the mixture into the bottom of the lightly greased 9x12 pan.

3. Place in 375F oven for 8 minutes.

4. In the meanwhile, place unwrapped caramels and remaining ⅓ cup evaporated milk in saucepan over low heat. Stir constantly to ensure caramels do not burn. Remove from heat once the caramels are melted.

5. Remove from pan oven. The mixture will not be cooked all the way through. Sprinkle 1 cup of chocolate chips over parbaked mixture. Pour the caramel mixture over the chips. Finally, sprinkle the rest of the cake mix mixture on top of the caramels.

6. Return pan to oven for 10-12 minutes until baked. Remove from oven. Let brownies stand until cooled. This allows the caramels to firm up before slicing.

Putting it all together:
7. Slice brownies into small squares and serve.

Evelyn's Lemon Icebox Pie

PREP TIME	REST TIME	MAKES
10 min	3 hrs-overnight	8

Momma makes the best icebox pie and makes it everytime I visit! It'll make you pucker up and love it!

INGREDIENTS
- Graham cracker pie crust
- 1 14oz can condensed milk
- ½ cup lemon juice
- Lemon zest (optional)
- 1 teaspoon vanilla extract
- 8 oz cream cheese softened
- 4 oz whipped topping
- Lemon slices (optional)

DIRECTIONS

1. Combine all ingredients except whipped topping and lemon zest. Beat until smooth.

2. Fold in whipped topping and lemon zest. Pour into pie crust.

3. Refrigerate overnight or place in freezer for a couple of hours to firm up

4. Add a couple of slices of lemon for garnish.

Chocolate Espresso Cake

PREP TIME	OVEN TEMP	COOK TIME	MAKES
15 min	400F	30 min	4

This dessert is so rich and coffee-chocolatey you will want to make this every day! But it's perfect for guests.

INGREDIENTS
- 3/4 cup all-purpose flour
- 2 tablespoon instant espresso powder
- 2 tablespoon cocoa powder
- 1½ teaspoon baking powder
- ¼ teaspoon salt
- ¼ cup unsalted butter, melted
- 1½ cup granulated sugar
- ¼ cup milk
- 1½ teaspoon vanilla extract
- 1 egg
- ¼ cup additional cocoa powder
- ⅓ cup light brown sugar
- ⅓ cup granulated sugar
- ¼ cup miniature chocolate chips
- 1¼ cups hot water

Whipped cream
Mint Sprig

EQUIPMENT
- 4 oven safe ramekins

DIRECTIONS

1. Pre-heat oven to 400F. Spray ramekins with vegetable oil and flour each.

2. Combine flour, espresso, cocoa, baking powder and salt in a bowl. Set aside.

3. In a separate bowl, whisk together melted butter, milk, vanilla and sugar. Then whisk in egg. Mix in flour mixture.

4. Pour mixture into 4 ramekins.

5. In a bowl, combine cocoa, sugars and chocolate chips. Pour hot water over mixture and stir until melted. Gently pour on top of flour mixture in ramekins. Do Not Stir or Mix.

5. Place ramekins on a cookie sheet and place in 400F oven for 25-30 minutes. Check doneness by inserting a toothpick until it comes out clean.

6. Let cake rest for 10 minutes. Then add whipped cream and a sprig of mint before serving.

Looking for the perfect topping?

Drizzle with coffee liquor and a scoop of vanilla ice cream.

Mixed Berry Crumble

⏰ PREP TIME	🔥 OVEN TEMP	⏱ COOK TIME	🍽 MAKES
15 min	400F	25 min	8

Fruit and delicious - the perfect complement for a large scoop of ice cream on a summer night!

INGREDIENTS

- 1½ cup blackberries
- 1½ cup raspberry
- 1½ cup strawberry, halved
- 1 cup sugar
- 1 tablespoon cornstarch
- 2 teaspoons lemon juice
- ⅛ teaspoon salt
- Lemon zest
- 1 teaspoon cinnamon (optional)
- 2 tablespoons butter
- Crumble topping (page 137)

EQUIPMENT

- Saucepan
- Casserole dish or individual ramekins (8)

DIRECTIONS

1. Heat saucepan over medium heat. Add berries, sugar, salt and cinnamon (optional). Stir and let berries cook down just a little.

2. Mix lemon juice with cornstarch and add to filling in saucepan. The sauce will start to thicken up. Turn off heat.

3. Pour filling into a lightly greased dish. Cut butter into small pieces and place on top of filling.

4. Generously sprinkle crumble topping. Bake in 400F oven for 25 min. Fruit should be tender. If crumble begins to brown too quickly, loosely cover with foil.

Fresh berries not available?

You can use frozen berries if needed. You can also substitute in some blueberries or even pitted cherries. Add cinnamon, allspice or cardamom for fall crumbles.

Crumble Topping

PREP TIME	OVEN TEMP	COOK TIME	MAKES
15 min	400F	25 min	8

Fruit and delicious - the perfect complement for a large scoop of ice cream on a summer night!

INGREDIENTS
- 1 cup all-purpose flour
- ½ cup packed brown sugar
- ½ teaspoon cinnamon
- ¼ teaspoon salt
- 1 stick unsalted butter

DIRECTIONS
1. Combine all dry ingredients in a bowl.

2. Using a box grater, grate butter into flour mixture.

3. Crumble the butter into the flour using a fork or pastry cutter. Leave a variety of butter sizes.

4. Use immediately or refrigerate in air tight container for 3 days.

Pie Crust

PREP TIME	REST TIME	MAKES
15 min	2 hours	2 - 9" crusts

INGREDIENTS
- 2½ cups flour
- 2 tablespoons sugar
- 1 teaspoon salt
- 2½ sticks COLD butter
- 6-8 tablespoons ice water

DIRECTIONS
Crust:
1. Combine flour, sugar and salt in a bowl. Using the large side of a grater, quickly grate the butter into flour.

2. Toss with a fork to fully distribute the butter. Add tablespoons of water until all the flour is incorporated. The dough should just come together but not be sticky. Form the dough into a ball.

3. Divide into two balls. Flatten each into a small disk. Wrap in plastic and refrigerate for 2 hours (or overnight).

Chocolate Chip Cookies

PREP TIME	OVEN TEMP	COOK TIME	MAKES
15 min	375F	10-12 min	36

You just think you know how to make chocolate chip cookies! These cookies are soft, chewy and all-around scrumptious perfection!

INGREDIENTS
- ¾ cup solid shortening
- 1½ cups packed brown sugar
- 2 tablespoon milk
- 4 teaspoon vanilla
- 1 egg plus 1 egg yolk
- 2-2¼ Cups all purpose flour
- 1 teaspoon salt
- ¾ teaspoon baking soda
- ½ teaspoon baking powder
- 1 cup semi-sweet chocolate chips

EQUIPMENT
- Mixer
- Cookie sheet

DIRECTIONS
1. Pre-Heat oven to 375F

2. In mixing bowl cream shortening and brown sugar, mixing on medium high speed until light and fluffy. Don't skip this step.

3. Add the milk and vanilla mixing on medium speed to incorporate. Add eggs and beat. Turn off mixer. Scrape sides and bottom of mixing bowl.

4. Add remaining dry ingredients (Flour, salt, baking soda and baking powder). Mix on low speed until fully mixed.

5. Stirring in by hand, add the chocolate chips.

6. Drop by rounded spoonfuls onto cookie sheet spacing apart about 2 inches. Cook in 375F oven for 10-12 minutes or until done.

Putting it together:

7. If you can get them onto a platter with being gobbled up, serve with cold milk.

Like a little more crunch in your cookie?

Try substituting granulated sugar for the brown sugar and you'll have all the crunch you want!

Black and White Mousse

PREP TIME 10 min   **REST TIME** 90 min   **MAKES** 4

This dessert is so simple and yet is always a hit. I mean, who doesn't like chocolate and whipped cream!

INGREDIENTS

Dark Chocolate Layer
- 2 cups heavy whipping cream
- 8 oz dark chocolate, chopped
- 1 teaspoon vanilla
- Pinch of salt

White Chocolate layer
- 1 cup heavy whipping cream
- 4 oz white chocolate, chopped
- ½ teaspoon vanilla
- Pinch of salt

Optional for richer mousse:
- 2 oz cream cheese, softened
- 1 tablespoon powdered sugar

EQUIPMENT
- 4 dessert dishes
- Mixer

DIRECTIONS

Dark layer:

1. Whip 1½ cup whipping cream in a glass bowl with mixer until stiff peaks form. Set aside.

2. Heat ½ cup whipping cream in microwave until hot but not boiling. Pour over dark chocolate and mix until chocolate melted. Add vanilla and salt.

3. Fold in whipped cream. Reserve ½ of mixture and refrigerate. Spoon remaining half into 4 individual dessert bowls and refrigerate for 30 minutes.

White layer:

4. Whip 3/4 cup whipping cream in a glass bowl with mixer until stiff peaks form. Set aside.

5. Heat 1/4 cup whipping cream in microwave until hot but not boiling. Pour over white chocolate and mix until chocolate melted. Add vanilla and salt. If adding cream cheese, beat with a mixer the cream cheese and powdered sugar until smooth. Add in the white chocolate mixture. Fold in the whipped cream.

6. Spoon on top of the chilled dark chocolate layer. Refrigerate for an additional 30 minutes.

7. Spoon remaining dark chocolate mousse on top of chilled white chocolate mousse. Chill until firm. Serve with pirouettes, additional dollop of whipped cream or chocolate curls.

Spice it up?

Try new flavors in your chocolate like espresso, cinnamon or cayenne pepper!

All-American Apple Pie

PREP TIME	OVEN TEMP	COOK TIME	SERVES
25 min	425F	30 min	8

Fruit and delicious - the All-American, perfect complement for a large scoop of ice cream on a summer night!

INGREDIENTS
- 2 pie crusts
- 6 large apples
- ½ cup brown sugar
- ¼ white sugar
- 3 tablespoons butter
- 1 lemon, juice and zest
- 1½ tablespoons cornstarch
- 3 teaspoons cinnamon
- ½ teaspoon nutmeg, divided
- 1 egg white, beaten

EQUIPMENT
- 9" pie pan
- Skillet

DIRECTIONS

1. Pre Heat oven to 425F. Make the crust (page 137) or use a store-bought crust. Roll out the dough and place into a 9" pie pan. On top of the crust, lay a piece of parchment paper and add a single layer of dry beans or granulated sugar. This will help keep the crust from puffing up.

2. Par bake crust for 8-10 minutes until sides start to turn light brown. Remove from oven and remove parchment and beans. Dock (poke with a fork) the crust and return to oven for another 5-8 minutes until crust starts to brown in center. Remove from oven.

3. While crust is baking, prepare the filling. Peel (optional) and slice apples into 1/4" slices and drizzle with juice. In a skillet, melt 1 tablespoon of butter. Add apples and toss with 1/4 cup white sugar, 1 teaspoon cinnamon and ¼ teaspoon nutmeg. Sauté the apples for about 4 minutes. They will not be soft yet.

4. Toss apples in bowl with cornstarch, brown sugar, 2 teaspoons cinnamon and ¼ teaspoon nutmeg. Add to parbaked crust. Dot with remaining butter and zest lemon over filling.

5. Roll out second pie crust. Cut into 3/4" wide strips. Lay strips horizontally across the top of the pie, spacing 3/4" apart. Lay additional strips vertically across the pie, weaving them over and under the horizontal strip. Trim off excess to edge of pie. Brush top and edges with egg white.

6. Bake for 15 minutes until crust turns brown and filling starts to bubble through top. Tent pie with aluminum foil if crust is browning too quickly.

Chocolate Caramel Torte

PREP TIME	OVEN TEMP	COOK TIME	MAKES
20 min	350F	30 min	8

Decadent! Perfect for a special ocassion or just to spice up a weeknight. Chocolate lovers beware!

INGREDIENTS
8 ounces unsweet chocolate
1 tablespoon unsalted butter
1 cup heavy cream
2 large eggs yolks
2 tablespoons sugar
1 tablespoon cocoa powder
¾ teaspoon espresso powder
1 teaspoon vanilla
¼ teaspoon salt
Pie Crust, par baked (page 137)

Salted Caramel Sauce
½ teaspoon corn syrup
¾ cup sugar
3 tablespoons water
¼ cup heavy cream
2 tablespoons butter
1 tablespoon vanilla
Pinch of sea salt

EQUIPMENT
9" pie pan
Sauce pan

DIRECTIONS

1. Heat heavy cream in a saucepan. Add Ad butter. When it melts, remove from heat and add chopped chocolate and sugar. Whisk until melted.

2. Beat egg yolks in a small bowl. Whip in a little of the chocolate mixture to temper the eggs. Add cocoa powder and espresso powder.. Then whip the egg mixture into the chocolate mixture until completely mixed. Stir in vanilla and salt.

3. Pour into a par-baked crust (recipe page 137). Bake in 350F oven for 25-30 minutes. The center will still jiggle a little. Let cool.

4. To make caramel sauce, in a small pot, combine sugar, water and corn syrup. It should look like wet sand. Cook over medium heat. Watch closely, without stirring. The sugars will start to caramelize, turning from white to yellow to a golden color. As soon as you see it looking "caramel" color, pull off the heat and whisk in heavy cream and butter. Once well combined, add in the vanilla.

5. Pour caramel sauce over cooled torte and sprinkle with sea salt. For extra pizzazz, drizzle with chocolate sauce and add some whipped cream.

Appendix

Measurements

EQUIVALENTS

3 teaspoons = 1 tablespoon
2 tablespoons = 1 ounce
2 ounces = 1/4 cup
2 cups = 1 pint
4 cups (2 pints) = 1 quart

4 quarts = 1 gallon
16 ounces = 1 pound
1 cup butter = 2 sticks butter
1/3 cup butter = 5 1/3 Tablespoons butter
Dash or pinch = less than 1/8 teaspoon

1 teaspoon Baking Powder	1/4 teaspoon baking soda + 1/2 teaspoon cream of tartar
1 cup Bread Crumbs	1 cup cracker crumbs or oats or matzo meal
1 cup Butter	1 cup shortening 7/8 cup vegetable oil
1 cup Buttermilk	7/8 cup milk + 1 tablespoon vinegar or lemon juice 1 cup yogurt
1 cup Half & Half	7/8 cup milk + 1 tablespoon butter
1 cup Heavy Cream	3/4 cup milk + 1/3 cup butter OR 1 cup evaporated milk
1 Egg	3 tablespoons mayonnaise OR 1/2 banana mashed + 1/2 teaspoon baking powder
1 tablespoon Fresh Herbs	1 teaspoon dried herbs
1 teaspoon lemon/lime juice	1 teaspoon vingear OR 1 teaspoon white wine

Conversion charts

OVEN TEMPERATURES

°C	°F
140	275
150	300
160	325
180	350
190	375
200	400
210	425
220	450
240	475

WEIGHTS

ounces	grams
1	25
2	50
3	75
4	110
5	150
6	175
7	200
8	225
9	250
10	275
11	315
12	350
13	365
14	400
15	425
16/1lb	450

VOLUMES

fluid ounces	millilitres
1	25
2	55
3	75
4	120
5	150
6	175
7	200
8	225
9	250
10	275
15	425
20/1 pint	570
1¼ pints	725
1½ pints	850
1¾ pints	1 litre

Temperatures

RECOMMENDED TEMPERATURE FOR DONENESS

Chicken	165 F
Pork	145 F
Beef	Will continue cook 5-10 F while resting
Ground Beef	145 F
Roast and Steak	
Rare	125 F
Medium Rare	135 F
Medium	145 F
Medium Well	150 F
Well Done	160 F
Fish	145 F
Bread	200 F
Leftovers	165 F

what now?

Sometimes the flavor just isn't right. But how do you fix it? Well, here's a few suggestions.

There are 5 main flavors that need to be balanced:

SALTY/SPICE/BITTER/SWEET/SOUR

TOO BITTER?

Add some saltiness:

- cheese
- soy sauce
- bacon
- tomato
- mushroom

TOO SWEET AND SALTY?

Add some Bitterness:

- Coffee
- Cocoa
- Kale/Spinach
- Broccoli
- Grapefruit

TOO SWEET?

Add some Spice:

- Hot Sauce
- Wasabi
- Arugula
- Radish
- Ginger
- Peppers

TOO SOUR, BITTER, SPICY?

Add some Sweetness:

- Sugar/honey/syrup/jams
- ketchup
- Carrots
- beets
- fruits
- peas
- squash
- Apple Cider Vinegar

TOO SWEET, SPICY, BITTER?

Add some Sourness:

- Citrus Juice
- Vinegars
- Tomato
- Yogurt
- Sour Cream

Recipe Index

A
American Tacos, 63
Apple Pie, 140
Asparagus, Balsamic, 34
Asparagus, Lemon Roasted, 35

B
Back Porch Breeze, 14, 15
Bacon Brussel Sprouts, 38
Balsamic Glaze, 16
Baked Chicken With Parmesan Crust, 115
Barbecue Beef Brisket, 99
BBQ Shrimp New Orleans Style, 93
Beef:
    American Tacos, 63
    Barbecue Beef Brisket, 99
    Roast Beef Dip Sandwiches, 97
    Grandma's Beef Chili, 61
    Herb-Crusted Steak, 125
    Meatballs For Spaghetti, 105
    Pepper Steak, 85
    Steak And Fries, 73
    Traditional Beef Stew, 59
Boston Cream Pie Cupcakes, 132
Bread:
    Cinnamon Challah, 46
    Dinner Biscuits, 42
    Dinner Rolls, 47
    French, 49
    Granny's Biscuits, 43
    Rosemary Quick Bread, 45
Broccoli Slaw, 25
Bruschetta, Roasted, 37
Buffalo Wings, 111

C
Caprese Kabaobs, 17
Caprese Salad, 27
Carmel Brownies, 133
Challah Bread, 46
Charcuterie Board, 14
Cheese Plate, 12
Chicken Creole With Grits, 69
Chicken Gumbo, 123
Chicken Lettuce Wraps, 75
Chicken Piccata, 71
Chicken Tortilla Soup, 67
Chicken:
    Baked Chicken & Parmesan, 115
    Buffalo Wings, 111
    Chicken Creole With Grits, 69
    Chicken Gumbo, 123
    Chicken Lettuce Wraps, 75
    Chicken Piccata, 71
    Chicken Tortilla Soup, 67
    Curried Chicken, 129
    Dippin' Chicken, 107
    Honey Mustard Chicken, 127
    Italian Chicken Pasta, 57
    Lemon Chicken, Roasted, 81
    Lemon Thyme Cream Sauce, 91
    Nashville-Style Hot Chicken, 101
    One Pan Chicken, 87
    Orange Chicken, 53
    Picante Chicken, 65
    Puff Pastry Chicken, 55
    Ramen Encrusted Chicken, 117
    Sesame Chicken And Noodles, 119
    Teriyaki Wings, 113
Chocolate Caramel Torte, 141
Chocolate Chip Cookies, 138
Chocolate Espresso Cake, 135
Crab Cakes, 83
Crumble Topping, 137
Cucumber Carrot Salad, 24
Curried Chicken, 129

D
Dalgona Coffee, 9
Dinner Biscuits, 42
Dinner Rolls, 47
Dippin' Chicken, 107

E
Easter Ham, 121

Recipe Index

F
French Bread, 49
Fried Rice, 39

G
Grandma's Beef Chili, 61
Granny's Biscuits, 43
Green Beans, Granny's, 33
Green Beans, Sautéd, 32

H
Herb-Crusted Steak, 125
Honey Mustard Chicken, 127

I
Italian Chicken Pasta, 57

L
Lemon Chicken, Roasted, 81
Lemon Icebox Pie, 134
Lemon Thyme Cream Sauce, 91

M
Meatballs For Spaghetti, 105
Mixed Berry Crumble, 136

N
Nashville-Style Hot Chicken, 101

O
Okra, Fried, 30
One Pan Chicken, 87
Orange Chicken, 53
Oven Roasted Broccoli, 37

P
Parmesan Crisps, 21
Pepper Steak, 85
Pesto Pizza Sauce, 79
Picante Chicken, 65
Pizza Dough, 77
Pie Crust, 137

Pizza Sauce, 78
Pork:
    Easter Ham, 121
    Southern Pork BBQ, 109
    Puff Pastry Chicken, 55

R
Ramen Encrusted Chicken, 117
Remoulade Sauce, 28
Roast Beef Dip Sandwiches, 97
Roasted Root Vegetables, 36
Rosemary Bread, 45
Rosemary Potatoes, 29

S
Salmon With Herbed Butter, 89
Seafood:
    BBQ Shrimp New Orleans Style, 93
    Classic Crab Cakes, 83
    Salmon With Herbed Butter, 89
    Talipia & Tomato Cream Sauce, 95
Sesame Chicken And Noodles, 119
Sherry Shallot Vinaigrette, 26
Southern Pork BBQ, 109
Spaghetti Sauce, 103
Spice Tea, 8
Squash, Sautéd, 31
Steak And Fries, 73
Sweet Tea, 6

T
Talipia & Tomato Cream Sauce, 95
Tea:
    Kathy's Fruit, 7
    Spice, 8
    Sweet, 6
Teriyaki Wings, 113
Tortelini Skewers, 23
Traditional Beef Stew, 59

W
Wings:
    Buffalo, 111
    Teriyaki, 113

Glossary

Vegetable Cuts

CHOPPED
Cut into large (3/4 inch) or medium (1/2 inch cubes)

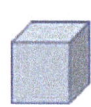

DICED
Cut into 1/4 inch cubes.

MINCED
Chop into very fine pieces 1/8-1/16 inch.

SLICED
Cutting into long even sized strips, generally 1/2 inch or wider

JULIENNE
Also called match stick - about 1/8 inch wide.

Terms

CREAM
To beat room temperature butter or shortening, to a light, fluffy consistency. This produces a lighter texture and a better volume.

DEGLAZE
To add liquid to a pan used to cook meat. After removing meat the liquid is added to the pan to help loosen the browned bits.

DREDGE
To coat a piece of food with dry ingredients like as flour or cornmeal

MARINADE
To soak food in a sauce. Add marinade to a plastic bag or bowl (not metal) and place in refrigerator for a period of time.

PARBOIL
To partially boil an item in order to produce a better end result when frying or baking food like potatoes.

PROOF
Time designated to allow yeast to work, causing bread to rise prior to baking. Should be done in a warm (80-100F) draft-free area

ROUX
A French term also in Cajun cooking. The process of browning flour and fat to a golden- or rich-brown color generally used as thickener.

SAUTÉ
To cook food over medium heat in a small amount of oil. This produces food with a caramelized surface.

ZEST
To use the peel of citrus fruit. Gently scraping with a microplane or fruit zester across the peel; a just until you see the pith (white part)

Photography Credits:

All Photographs were taken by Lance McAlindon

Except the following,:
Courtesy of Canva.com
    Pages 13, 15, 22, 23, 40, 51, 130, 142-146
Licensed from Envato
    Page 58, 120
Courtesy of unsplash.com
    Opening Page 1: Hannah Busing
    Opening Page 2: Lee Myungseong
    Page 6: Bady Abbas
    Page 9: Shreyak Singh
    Page 24: Roni Herdyanzah
    Page 36: American Heritage chocolate
    Page 50: Mona Monsoumi
    Page 98: Katerina Jerabkova

THANK YOU

Melinda McAlindon is brand and marketing strategist for consumer products and entertainment industries. She has an MBA from Indiana University and degrees in Engineering, Economics and Mathematics from Vanderbilt University. She is currently pursuing a degree at Brightwater Culinary School. Melinda and her husband Lance live together with their four children in Centerton, Arkansas.

www.ingramcontent.com/pod-product-compliance
Lightning Source LLC
Chambersburg PA
CBHW051256110526
44589CB00025B/2849